Middle East
Sources

Other books by Ian Richard Netton

Allah Transcendent
Studies in the Structure and Semiotics of Islamic Philosophy,
Theology and Cosmology

Arabia and the Gulf: From Traditional Society to Modern States
(*Editor*)

Al-Farabi and His School

Golden Roads: Migration, Pilgrimage and Travel in
Mediaeval and Modern Islam
(*Editor*)

Middle East Materials in United Kingdom and Irish Libraries
A Directory

Muslim Neoplatonists
An Introduction to the Thought of the Brethren of Purity

A Popular Dictionary of Islam

Seek Knowledge
Thought and Travel in the House of Islam

Text and Trauma
An East–West Primer

Middle East Sources

A MELCOM Guide to Middle Eastern and Islamic Books and Materials in United Kingdom and Irish Libraries

Compiled and Edited by

IAN RICHARD NETTON

Professor of Arabic Studies
University of Leeds

Routledge
Taylor & Francis Group

LONDON AND NEW YORK

First published 1998
by Curzon Press

2 Park Square, Milton Park, Abingdon, Oxon OX14 4RN
711 Third Avenue, New York, NY 10017, USA

*Routledge is an imprint of the Taylor & Francis Group,
an informa business*

First issued in paperback 2016

Typeset in Stone by LaserScript, Mitcham, Surrey

British Library Cataloguing in Publication Data
A catalogue record for this book is available from the British Library

Library of Congress Cataloging in Publication Data
A catalogue record for this book has been requested

ISBN 978-1-138-98104-1 (pbk)
ISBN 978-0-7007-1029-4 (hbk)

DEDICATION

For Audrey and Malcolm with love

Contents

Preface

The predecessor of this volume, *Middle East Materials in United Kingdom and Irish Libraries: A Directory* (London: Library Association Publishing), appeared in 1983. It is clear from comments received that it has been of considerable use to a wide body of readers including librarians, scholars, students and many others with an interest in the Middle East. The volume presented here, *Middle East Sources*, is much more than just a revised and enlarged edition of *Middle East Materials*. Much has changed in the world of libraries and librarianship since 1983. The old polytechnics have been renamed universities, new technology has enhanced the speed of communications and the 'death of the book' is increasingly mooted! In the light of all this, many entries from *Middle East Materials* have been rewritten, new ones have been added, and defunct libraries or schemes have been omitted. The Bibliography has been enlarged.

Generally speaking, each entry in this volume incorporates information on the address of the institution, its telephone, fax, e-mail and other numbers, a brief description of the collection with reference to relevant catalogues where useful, and to other directories, the number of items in the collection where known and a note on access. If the library or institution belongs to the MELCOM Area Specialisation Scheme (MASS), this is also noted and the relevant countries are listed. The omission of times of opening and closing is deliberate: this is one of the areas in any directory which is likely to change quickly and make that directory more dated than it might otherwise be. The interested reader is urged to phone or fax the library or institution which he or she desires to use *before* any visit, to ascertain the current opening hours.

As before, information was collected by means of questionnaires and the editor-compiler was very much dependant on the goodwill of busy librarians and information officers for the completion of these and, indeed, for the length and quality of information offered under the rubric 'brief description'. Some institutions took the opportunity to send much larger quantities of information than were actually requested. Where it was thought that this might be of use to the reader, such information has been incorporated, as in the three Appendices. It is hoped that this procedure will not make the present Directory appear either lopsided in emphasis or downright idiosyncratic! Much *has* been edited out where it was felt to be irrelevant or of no use to the reader or user of this manual.

A major feature of the compilation of the Directory was that a questionnaire was sent to every one of the new universities (i.e. the former polytechnics). Generally, the response rate was very poor: some stated simply that they had no relevant holdings while large numbers of others did not bother to reply. This should not, of course, be taken as a signal that the majority of former polytechnics do not have any holdings of Middle Eastern materials at all.

This Directory surveys mainly libraries and archives but some museums with interesting material have been included as well. It does not claim to be a complete and comprehensive survey of Britain's and Ireland's very rich Middle Eastern collections but simply to present a pocket-sized, representative selection of sources to which both student and scholar may have recourse.

I am grateful to MELCOM for suggesting that *Middle East Materials* should be updated. I am proud to record that I have been a member of MELCOM since 1975, my interest in matters bibliographical having been aroused during my career as the first Assistant Librarian (Arabic Specialist) at the University of Exeter from 1975 to 1977. While I have moved on to other academic pastures, my interest in, and affection for, librarianship remains. I hope that this volume will provide a further useful contribution to the field of Middle Eastern reference studies.

Ian Richard Netton
Professor of Arabic Studies
University of Leeds
December 1996

Foreword

MELCOM (UK) was founded in 1967, at the same time as most area studies library groups, as a direct outgrowth of the Hayter Committee. This committee had been set up to look into the state of Oriental, Slavonic, East European and African studies and reported to Parliament in 1961, recommending that 'interested universities should set up committees covering Oriental, African and Slavonic library needs', mainly with a view to improved acquisition, cooperation and shared cataloguing. The Middle East Libraries Committee or MELCOM (as it was then called) was formed precisely to improve cooperation among the libraries collecting vernacular language material in the area of its interests, which were (and remain) all Arabic-speaking countries, Iran, Afghanistan, Central Asia (Turkic material), Turkey and the Ottoman Empire and Islamic Studies. Hebrew, Judaic and Israeli Studies are the province of the Hebraica Libraries Group.

MELCOM (UK) has always enjoyed the support of all national, university and special libraries actively collecting on the Middle East. The Committee has never had a formal membership structure, but is open to all interested parties who feel they can contribute to its stated aims. During its almost thirty-year existence, MELCOM has had members who are librarians, archivists, documentalists, bibliographers, academics (among its distinguished chairmen have been Professor Bob Serjeant, Professor Derek Latham and Dr. Derek Hopwood), members of the book trade and several private scholars.

At the Committee's twice-yearly meetings, cooperation has always dominated discussion. The Committee has always been more than just a forum for debate, however, and among its concrete achievements can be listed:

- Contributing records to the Union Catalogue of Asian Publications (UCAP), until the virtual demise of the card catalogue rendered this activity obsolete;
- Establishing and monitoring an area specialisation scheme to ensure both that no country of the Middle East was neglected bibliographically, and, conversely, that unnecessary duplication

did not take place. Particular attention has always been given to newspapers, periodicals and official publications, but since the scheme has always been informal, the agreed guidelines have been subject to the vagaries of changing academic policy within each institution. The overall structure of shared collection development has, however, more or less stood the test of time;

- Promoting the use of standard transliteration schemes for all the major Middle Eastern languages;
- Setting up and contributing to a special section of the *British Journal of Middle Eastern Studies* (formerly, the *British Society for Middle Eastern Studies Bulletin*) reserved for reviews of Bibliographies and Works of Reference, and related bibliographical articles;
- Instituting an e-mail discussion list for matters pertaining to Middle East librarianship and bibliography; the list, called lis-middle-east@mailbase.ac.uk was set up in July 1995;
- Cooperating with European libraries with similar aims to British institutions. To this end, MELCOM arranged ten conferences in nine different cities between 1979 and 1988, at which point MELCOM International was formed, and the practice of annual conferences has continued under its auspices;
- Lastly, but perhaps most importantly, MELCOM (UK) has been active in the field of publishing a wide variety of bibliographical aids to Middle Eastern studies. These have ranged from three separate directories of periodicals and newspapers in British libraries in Arabic, in Persian, and Turkish and Turkic, through individual bibliographical guides to the Arab world and Iran to guides to Middle Eastern photographic collections in the UK, bibliographies of Arabic bibliographical dictionaries and an introduction to book selection from the Arab world. Some of these have appeared with commercial publishers, but most have been issued under MELCOM (UK)'s own imprint.

One of the most important projects which MELCOM (UK) supported was the first edition of Ian Netton's *Middle East Materials in United Kingdom and Irish Libraries: A Directory* (1983). This was the first time such a comprehensive work of its kind had appeared and it brought to light an enormous wealth of Middle Eastern materials housed in the widest possible variety of libraries – public, private, national, university, polytechnic, diplomatic and special. With its lucid organization and detailed description of contents, it has remained the *vade-mecum* not only of all MELCOM (UK) members, but of anyone intent on pursuing serious scholarship on the Middle East in Britain. This succeeding volume has been entirely reset and revised, has many new and expanded entries, and includes new kinds of information (eg fax numbers and e-mail addresses), but still manages to retain the easy-to-use format of the original. All scholars and students will be grateful to Professor Netton for agreeing to update an invaluable work with his usual meticulous scholarship and attention to detail. The Directory represents an excellent example of the cooperation between academics and librarians, which is the bedrock upon which MELCOM (UK) was founded, and which remains one of its guiding principles.

Paul Auchterlonie
Chairman MELCOM (UK)
University of Exeter Library
April 1996

Abbreviations

Auch.	Paul Auchterlonie (ed.), *Collections in British Libraries on Middle Eastern and Islamic Studies*, Occasional Papers Series No. 12, (Durham: University of Durham Centre for Middle Eastern and Islamic Studies, 1982).
BNB	*British National Bibliography.*
Browne	Edward G. Browne, *A Hand-list of the Muhammadan Manuscripts, Including All Those Written in the Arabic Character, Preserved in the Library of the University of Cambridge*, (Cambridge: Cambridge University Press, 1900).
Browne (Supp.)	Edward G. Browne, *A Supplementary Hand-list of the Muhammadan Manuscripts, Including All Those Written in the Arabic Character, Preserved in the Libraries of the University and Colleges of Cambridge*, (Cambridge: Cambridge University Press, 1922).
BSOAS	*Bulletin of the School of Oriental and African Studies.*
IDC	Inter-Documentation Company.
Jones	Philip Jones, *Britain and Palestine 1914–1918: Archival Sources for the History of the British Mandate*, (Oxford: Published for the British Academy by the OUP, 1979).
JRAS	*Journal of the Royal Asiatic Society.*
JSS	*Journal of Semitic Studies.*
MASS	MELCOM Area Specialisation Scheme.
MEED	*Middle East Economic Digest.*
Morgan	Paul Morgan, *Oxford Libraries outside the Bodleian: A Guide*, (Oxford: Oxford Bibliographical Society and the Bodleian Library, 1973).
Munby	A.N.L. Munby, *Cambridge College Libraries*, 2nd edn., (Cambridge: W. Heffer & Sons, 1962).
MWP	Noel Matthews, M. Doreen Wainwright & J.D. Pearson, *A Guide to Manuscripts and Documents in the British Isles Relating to the Middle East and North Africa*, (Oxford: OUP, 1980).

Pearson	J.D. Pearson, *Oriental Manuscripts in Europe and North America: A Survey*, Bibliotheca Asiatica 7, (Zug, Switzerland: Inter-Documentation Company, 1971).
Roman	Stephan Roman, *The Development of Islamic Library Collections in Western Europe and North America*, (London & New York: Mansell, 1990).
Roper 2	Geoffrey Roper (ed.), *World Survey of Islamic Manuscripts Volume II*, (London: Al-Furquan Islamic Heritage Foundation, 1993).
Roper 3	Geoffrey Roper (ed.), *World Survey of Islamic Manuscripts Volume III*, (London: Al-Furqan Islamic Heritage Foundation, 1994).
Roper 4	Geoffrey Roper (ed.), *World Survey of Islamic Manuscripts Volume IV (Supplement)*, (London: Al-Furqan Islamic Heritage Foundation, 1994).
SCOLMA	Standing Conference of Library Materials on Africa.
SOAS	School of Oriental and African Studies, University of London.

MELCOM Area Specialisation Scheme (MASS)

Participating Libraries attempt to collect in depth in the following areas:

1) Specialised monographs on modern (post 1800) studies.
2) Pamphlets.
3) Party political publications.
4) Newspapers.
5) Vernacular periodicals.

The following kinds of material are in general not collected:

1) Official gazettes (collected by the British Library, Durham Documentation Unit and SOAS).
2) Laws and law reports (collected by the British Library and SOAS).
3) Parliamentary debates (not issued).
4) Specialised statistical material (collected by Durham Documentation Unit for the whole Middle East, by Exeter Documentation Unit for the Arabian Peninsula and by SOAS for North Africa).

Individual countries and areas of the Middle East have been divided among MELCOM Libraries as follows:

Arabian Peninsula:	Cambridge, Exeter (Exeter does not collect extensively vernacular periodicals or works of literature), British Library
Iran:	SOAS, Middle East Centre (Oxford)
Iraq:	Exeter (Monographs only)
Israel:	SOAS, Middle East Centre (Oxford), Oxford Centre for Hebrew and Jewish Studies
Jordan, Lebanon:	British Library, Middle East Centre (Oxford)
Libya:	Middle East Centre (Oxford)
North Africa:	SOAS
Sudan:	Durham
Syria:	British Library
Turkey:	SOAS

Users' Notes

Because they are among the first things to change in any Directory like this, opening and closing times for the institutions listed in this volume are not given. Prospective users are advised to telephone for such details in advance of their visit.

Bibliographical information in each entry is given in abbreviated form. Full details (publisher, date of publication etc.) for each book or article cited will be found in the *Bibliography* at the back of the Directory.

Directory

ABERDEEN

Aberdeen University Library ■

Address:	Aberdeen University Library,
	Queen Mother Library,
	Meston Walk,
	Aberdeen AB9 2UE
Address:	Department of Special Collections and Archives,
	Aberdeen University Library,
	King's College,
	Aberdeen AB9 2UB
Tel:	Main Library: 01224 272579
	Dept. of Special Collections and Archives: 01224 272598
Fax:	01224 487048
e-mail:	library@abdn.ac.uk
	speclib@aberdeen.ac.uk
Janet:	abdn.lib

There is no separate department of Islamic Studies in the University, but Hebrew and Arabic with some other Semitic languages are taught in the Department of Divinity with Religious Studies to honours level. The main library houses the more modern and heavily used texts for the current teaching of Hebrew and Arabic, under the respective Dewey subject classification numbers, but there is no separate collection of works for Arabic or Islamic Studies. In the library as a whole there are c.800 vols. relating to Islamic Studies, c.1000 vols. relating to Jewish religion and history, c.500 vols. relating to Hebrew language and literature, c.500 vols. relating to Arabic language and literature and c.200 vols. relating to other Middle Eastern languages.

Until the fusion in 1860 there were two Universities in Aberdeen: King's College, founded in 1495, and Marischal College founded in 1593. The current Chair of Hebrew and Semitic Languages derives from the Chair of Hebrew at King's College established in 1673, and that of Oriental Languages at Marischal established in 1732. Books in Hebrew and other Middle Eastern languages have been in the Library since the foundation of the University and acquired continually.

The Department of Special Collections and Archives holds the books from the two ancient University Libraries, the main sequences of which are arranged in Dewey order. Among these collections are many items relevant to the study of Hebrew and Arabic along with Old Testament Studies. There are many printed versions of the Hebrew Bible, dated from the 15th Century. There is also a manuscript version of the Hebrew Bible (MS 23) dated 1493, written in a Sephardic hand and probably from Naples. The Department of Special Collections and Archives also has a collection of 231 incunabula, some 15 of which are translations of Arabic texts, mainly concerned with science, mathematics and astronomy.

In the Department there are many individually named Special Collections which are of relevance: the Biesenthal Collection contains c.2000 vols., c.800 of which are in Hebrew or Hebrew characters representing virtually the whole published output in Hebrew up to the year 1872. The non-Hebrew works are mainly in German, ranging from 17th Century works through to the 19th Century.

The papers of Major Malcolm Hay of Seaton (1881–1962) (MS 2788) are deposited in the University Archives. He was sympathetic to the Zionist movement and some of his correspondence to his associates in Israel is in Hebrew. The Collection also contains some modern Hebrew texts.

The Wilson Collection consists of both manuscript and printed items. Robert Wilson travelled extensively to the Near and Middle East, building up a collection of books on the archaeology, history and travel of these areas. His diaries and notebooks also exist in manuscript form.

Access: The Library is open to the public for reference, but borrowing is limited to students, staff and external members. The majority of the material housed in the Department of Special Collections and Archives is for consultation only, and usually some notice is required since many items have to be fetched from store.

See: Auch. pp. 78–80, Jones p. 216, MWP p. 352, Pearson pp. 61, 145, 319, Roman p. 49, Roper 3 pp. 436–437.

ABERYSTWYTH

The Hugh Owen Library, University of Wales, Aberystwyth   ■

Address:	The Hugh Owen Library,
	University of Wales,
	Aberystwyth,
	Penglais,
	Aberystwyth,
	Dyfed SY23 3RZ
Tel:	01970 622391
Fax:	01970 622404
e-mail:	library@aber.ac.uk

The Library's holdings in Islamic and Middle Eastern material are incorporated in the main book collection. The larger collections are as follows:

– History, geography and international relations of the Middle East: c.2500 titles
– History, geography and international relations of Islamic North Africa: c.530 titles
– Islamic philosophy and religion: c.500 titles
– Middle Eastern language and literature: c.300 titles

A number of sources of current information relevant to Islamic and Middle Eastern Studies (e.g. *Times, Guardian, Keesing's Record of World Events*) are accessible by CD-ROM.

Access: Access is available to staff and students of the University. Other scholars and researchers may be permitted to use the Library for reference use only on application to the Librarian.

See: Pearson p. 482, Roper 3 p. 438.

National Library of Wales   ■

Address:	National Library of Wales,
	Aberystwyth,
	Dyfed SY23 3BU
Tel:	01970 623816
Fax:	01970 615709

There are no specific and separately housed Islamic or Middle Eastern collections of books. There are also no *special* collections of Islamic or Middle Eastern manuscripts. However, see the catalogues listed below.

There are a large number of personal and estate collections, described in typescript catalogues, which contain scattered items mainly relating to India. The references to these items may be ascertained from Indexes available in the Manuscript Reading Room. There are two collections which contain substantial groups of material, viz. *The Clive Mss and Papers*, which contain the journals, correspondence and papers of Robert, Lord Clive (1725–1774) and Edward (Clive), Earl of Powis (1754–1839), and *The Kentchurch Court Papers and Documents*, which contain the letters and papers of Sir Harford Jones, afterwards Sir Harford Jones Brydges, Bart. (1764–1847), who served with the East India Company and became the first British ambassador to Persia.

Approximate numbers of books: There are three principal categories of books relative to Islamic and Middle Eastern Studies:

(a) Historical, geographical and descriptive: c.1000 vols. Some are 19th Century but most are 20th Century imprints. There is also much on the Arab Gulf.

(b) Languages and literatures of the Middle East: c.2000 vols. Imprints range from the 17th to the 20th centuries. The one important private collection is the T. Witton Davies bequest, the source of many 19th Century works in French, German and English. Important sub-groups are:

(1) Hebrew grammar and lexicography: c.300 vols.

(2) Arabic grammar and lexicography: c.250 vols.

(3) Persian language and literature: c.250 vols.

(c) Islamic religion: c.1000 vols. These are mostly legal deposit books. The Witton Davies Bequest (1923) includes some 30 vols. of Semitic material. Editions of the Qur'an include the first Arabic edition, edited by Hinkelman and published at Hamburg in 1694, and *The Alkoran*, translated into English by Sieur Du Ryer and published in London in 1949.

Access: Access is available to the public.

See: Jones p. 223, MWP pp. 347–350, Pearson pp. 118, 482, Roman pp. 49–50, Roper 3 pp. 437–438.

See also: Herman Ethé, *A Catalogue of Oriental Manuscripts, Persian, Arabic and Hindustani*; National Library of Wales, *Handlist of Manuscripts in the National Library of Wales*; [Typed] *Handlist of Mss in the NLW in or Relating to the Semitic Languages* (this was compiled in 1972 but practically all the manuscripts which it lists have been described in the *Handlist of Manuscripts in the National Library of Wales*).

University of Wales, Aberystwyth, Library ∎

See under: ABERYSTWYTH: The Hugh Owen Library.

BATH

■ Bath University Library

Address:	University of Bath Library,
	Claverton Down,
	Bath BA2 7AY
Tel:	01225 826835 (General enquiries desk)
Fax:	01225 826229

The Islamic and Middle East collections at Bath are not extensive. Holdings relate mainly to the now-defunct MA course in Translation and Linguistics for Arabic speakers, and are in the field of Arabic literature with some peripheral holdings in the politics, economics and institutions of the Arabic-speaking world. Since the MA course folded in the early 1990s there has been no addition to the Islamic holdings, and there are currently no plans to restart Islamic Studies at Bath.

Access: Any bona fide user has access to the Library. Prospective users are advised to phone before visiting, to ascertain whether the stock is suitable to their needs.

BELFAST

Central Library, Belfast   ■

Address:	Central Library,
	Belfast Public Libraries,
	Royal Avenue,
	Belfast BT1 1EA
Tel:	01232 243233
Fax:	01232 332819
Telex:	747359

The Central Library holds a good general collection of reference books and monographs covering the history, geography, art, language and literature of the Middle East. All United Nations Publications are also held on file.

Access: Everyone is entitled to use the reference collection and some titles are available for loan.

Public Record Office of Northern Ireland   ■

Address:	Public Record Office of Northern Ireland,
	66, Balmoral Avenue,
	Belfast BT9 6NY
Tel:	01232 251318
Fax:	01232 255999

The major holding of material relating to the Middle East, and, more specifically, colonial administration, in the Public Record Office of Northern Ireland (hereafter PRONI), is to be found in the Dufferin Papers (PRONI ref. D.1071) relating to the career of Frederick, 1st Marquis of Dufferin and Ava in Syria, 1860–1863, and Egypt, 1879–1883. Many of PRONI's other private collections also have references to administrative service abroad. In addition, Irish regiments were involved in Middle East Campaigns. One such is the Royal Irish Fusiliers (PRONI ref. 3574). The papers include those of individual soldiers: a diary of the Sudan expedition kept by Brevet-Major D.W. Churcher, illustrated with photographs, cartoons and newspaper cuttings, 1898; and also diaries and letters written from Palestine,

1898–1900 and 1917–1918. This material, while interesting, is unfortunately small in volume (see APPENDIX ONE).

A more significant collection, in volume, is the Pollock Papers (PRONI ref. D.1581). J.H.H. Pollock served as a Lieutenant, Captain and Major in the 6th Royal Irish Rifles during the First World War; in OETA Palestine, 1919–1920; as District Commissioner to Haifa, 1939; to Jerusalem, 1944–1948; and as Chief Advisor to the GOC British Troops in Palestine, 1948. The papers include c.300 letters, diaries, notebooks and files. There are also a file of reports, and c.50 letters addressed to Mrs. Pollock as Vice-President of the Red Cross in Haifa, 1940–1942, and subsequently for the Jerusalem district (see APPENDIX ONE). Another collection of note concerns the life and career of General Francis Chesney, Kilkeel, Co. Down (PRONI ref. D.3480), and, in particular, an expedition which he led to the Euphrates Valley, 1830–1831. The papers include an autobiographical narrative of Chesney's travel to Turkey, Egypt, Lebanon, Syria etc. (see APPENDIX ONE).

Access: Generally access is unrestricted to private collections deposited in the PRONI. In this context the term 'private' is used to define a document that did not originate with an official body. However, there are certain exceptions:

(1) Access may be restricted in accordance with terms laid down by the depositor.
(2) A collection may be closed for purposes of conservation or archival processing.

Potential users are strongly urged to get in touch with the PRONI *in advance* to ascertain if the material they are interested in will be available.

See: Jones pp. 203, 223, MWP pp. 376–384, and APPENDIX ONE of this volume.

■ Queen's University of Belfast Library

Address:	The Library,
	The Queen's University of Belfast,
	Belfast BT7 1LS
Tel:	01232 245133
Fax:	01232 323340
e-mail:	(Main Library information desk) lbg0043@qub.ac.uk

The basis of the Library's present Persian and Arabic collections was a selection from the oriental library of Professor Charles MacDouall (Professor of Greek, 1850–1878), which was purchased by his friends and admirers and presented to the Library in 1879. The University has offered courses in Semitic Studies since 1967. Approximate numbers of books: History, geography, economics, politics, sociology, law 2000 titles; Literature 1200; Islam 500; Judaism 1100; Old Testament 2000; Science, philosophy 125; Music, art 70. Special items worthy of mention include c.200 Persian and Arabic titles (principally European editions) of the 17th to the early 19th centuries from the MacDouall Collection; the Ross-Rosenzweig Collection largely on the Dead Sea Scrolls; and 53 Persian manuscripts of the 17th and 18th centuries (poetry and stories, history and geography, ethics and Sufism, epistolary guides and grammars, medicine and cookery).

Access: Non-members of the University may consult materials at the Librarian's discretion; borrowing rights are available on payment of an annual fee.

See: MWP p. 384, Roper 3 pp. 439–440.

BIRMINGHAM

■ Birmingham Museum and Art Gallery

Address: Birmingham Museum and Art Gallery,
                Chamberlain Square,
                Birmingham B3 3DH
Tel: 0121 235 4201
Fax: 0121 236 6227

The Middle Eastern Collections of the Department of Archaeology and Ethnography are purely ancient, i.e. pre-Islamic. There is a small library of some 500 volumes on ancient Near Eastern and ancient Egyptian archaeology; very few textual and philological works are stocked.

Access: The Museum and Art Gallery are open to the general public. The *library* is intended only to assist in the curation of the Museum collections and is not a formal research library. As such it is only accessible to members of staff and to visiting scholars and students working on items in the Museum collections.

■ Central Library, Selly Oak Colleges

Address: The Central Library,
                Selly Oak Colleges,
                Birmingham B29 6LQ
Tel: 0121 472 4231
Fax: 0121 472 8852

The Islamic collection began with the manuscripts collected in the Near East by Dr. Alphonse Mingana in the 1920s at Dr. Edward Cadbury's expense. The books and periodicals were first collected to supplement and support the manuscripts collection, but now serve the much wider readership of the Centre for the Study of Islam and Muslim–Christian Relations within the Colleges, and from the University of Birmingham. There is also a fast growing Centre for the Documentation of Islam in Europe. The Library covers the whole range of Islamic countries in all their aspects and possesses all the classical texts of Islam. There is a section on the Arab Gulf (though not much on the present commercial and technological aspects). The modern Islamic books are catalogued within the computerised catalogue of the Library. For the Catalogue of the Mingana Mss Collection, see below.

Approximate numbers of books: In European languages c.10,000; Arabic texts c.3000; Periodicals c.130 titles; Related serials to the Documentation of Islam in Europe project c.50; Manuscripts – see Catalogues; Arabic papyri and paper fragments c.400 items. The American Theological Library Association Religion Database, and the Library of Congress Bibliographic Database are available on CD-ROM.

Access: Access to the collections is open to all staff and students from the Colleges. Interested scholars can gain access by appointment. There is a Summer School when the Library is open to participants from all over the world.

See: Pearson pp. 60, 92, 118, 145, 173, 185, 317, Roman pp. 39–40, Roper 3 pp. 441–443.
See also: *Catalogue of the Mingana Collection of Manuscripts*, (for full details of this, see *sv* Mingana, A. in the Bibliography). Vols. 1–3 are now out of print. The *Catalogue* has been made available *in microfiche* by the Inter-Documentation Company AG.

BOSTON SPA

■ **British Library Document Supply Centre**

Address:	British Library Document Supply Centre, Boston Spa, Wetherby, West Yorkshire LS23 7BQ
Tel:	01937 546060
Fax:	01937 546333
e-mail:	customer-services@bl.uk

Founded in 1973 (though much earlier stock is held), the collection covers all subjects and all countries including over 236,000 journal titles (49,000 currently received), over 3 million books, nearly 4 million reports on microform, over 40,000 UK theses, over 100,000 US theses and over 300,000 conference proceedings, British official publications etc. There are also reports from international/national governmental organisations (NASA, EC etc.).

Modern works in English relating to the Middle East and Islam are bought extensively, provided they are of interest to customers in research, higher education or business. However, no information is available as to the size of the book collection exclusively concerned with these subjects.

Access: Borrowing by individuals is not permitted but is available to institutions who are registered as customers with BLDSC. Registration is generally required for other services (photocopy etc.) but an 'Easy-Order' service exists for non-registered customers. Payment is generally by prepaid loan or photocopy request forms/numbers. Access by post or Automated Request Transmission is available for registered customers. Unrestricted access exists to the Reading Room.

BRADFORD

Bradford and Ilkley Community College Library ■

See under: BRADFORD: Grove Library, Bradford and Ilkley Community College.

Central Library, Bradford ■

Address: Central Library,
           Prince's Way, Bradford,
           West Yorkshire BD1 1NN
Tel: 01274 753600
Fax: 01274 395108

English language material on Islam and the Middle East is part of the general Library bookstock and can be found via on-line public cataloguing terminals. This Library is particularly strong in Urdu material. It also takes the Arabic daily newspaper *al-Sharq al-Awsat* and the fortnightly news magazine, *Crescent International*.

   Approximate numbers of books: Islam 310; Urdu books on Islam 1500; the Middle East 450; related subjects (Islamic art, architecture, travel in the region) 400; telephone and trade directories 20.

Access: Apart from some reference material, all items may be borrowed by registered library users or borrowed through the Inter-Library Loan network.

Grove Library, Bradford and Ilkley Community College ■

Address: Department of Library and Learning Resources,
           Grove Building,
           Bradford and Ilkley Community College,
           Great Horton Road,
           Bradford,
           West Yorkshire BD7 1AY
Tel: 01274 753331

The Grove Library covers the following subject areas: Art and Design; Business and Social Studies; Humanities and Languages; Science and Technology. It also has a Multicultural Information

Centre which has books and periodicals dealing with: Race, Equality and Multicultural issues such as Feminism, Equality for Women, Ethnic Minorities and the Disabled, Multicultural Education in Schools, as well as information on Religious Customs and Cultures in other parts of the world.

Access: The College libraries are principally designed to support students and staff in their academic work. Prospective borrowers should complete a library membership form.

BRIGHTON

Brighton Reference Library   ■

Address: Brighton Reference Library,
           Church Street, Brighton,
           East Sussex BN1 1UE
Tel: 01273 691195–7

The best books in the Library are contained in two collections: the Long Collection and the Mathews Collection. The first comprises about 3500 books belonging to Professor Long of Brighton College and includes many rare classical texts dating from the 16th Century to 1870. The second comprises about 4000 books belonging to H.J. Mathews, an oriental scholar, and includes many early books in Hebrew, Syriac, Arabic and other Middle Eastern languages, dating from the 15th Century to 1900. In addition, the Library has a large collection of travel books, predominantly dated 1750–1830, many of which deal with the Middle East. There are also a small number of volumes (mainly translations but some original texts) containing Middle Eastern secular literature mainly dated between 1800–1920.

The Library has a small number of official reports, descriptions and maps of Middle Eastern countries mainly dated between 1900–1930, and also a fair collection of modern dictionaries and business directories of the Middle East.

Approximate numbers of books: There are no manuscripts but there are about 12,000, mainly early, books dated 1500–1820. These include, very approximately: Hebrew texts 3000; Arabic, Aramaic, Syriac etc. 2000; Travel, description and history (in English) of the Middle East 3000.

Access: The Library is open to all by visit, telephone or post.

See: MWP p. 228.

■   ## British Library for Development Studies

Address:	British Library for Development Studies,
	Institute of Development Studies,
	University of Sussex,
	Falmer,
	Brighton BN1 9RE
Tel:	01273 606261
Fax:	01271 621202/691647
Telex:	877997 IDSBTN G
e-mail:	blds@sussex.ac.uk
Devline:	See below under **Access**

The British Library for Development Studies (BLDS) began in 1966. Its collection comprises documents and publications in European languages relating to the socio-economic and political developments of most countries in Africa, Asia and Latin America and their relations with rich countries and the international community. Publications on Islam, as it affects the economy or society of these regions, are collected. The Middle East material includes primary documents from many Arab organisations and Middle East regional offices of international agencies; government documents (especially statistics) from all countries of the region; non-official publications especially from financial and commercial institutions and from educational establishments in the area; and a wide, if selective, range of similar materials about the region produced by counterpart institutions in other countries. Documents in Arabic or Hebrew are not collected. Similarly, newspapers are not collected. Approximately 2000 new titles relating to the Arab countries of the Middle East and North Africa have been added since 1988.

Access: Access to the Library is available to any bona fide reader.

– The post-1988 catalogue of the BLDS is available on the World Wide Web at http://www.ids.ac.uk.
– Devline: The Library runs a service called Devline which stands for Development Information Service Online. Devline serves all those with an interest in economic and social development, focusing on the relationships between rich and poor countries. It is a free public service available through Janet (the UK Joint Academic Network) and the Internet (the world-wide network of computer networks). Connecting to Devline:

- WWW: http://www.ids.ac.uk
- GOPHER: gopher://gopher.ids.ac.uk
- FTP: ftp://ftp.ids.ac.uk
- TELNET: telnet://info.ids.ac.uk
  (login: lynx *no password*)

Or connect via major gateway services.

Please contact Devline if you need instructions for WWWmail, Gophermail or Ftpmail. A direct telephone dial-up connection to selected Devline services can be arranged if required. Also, an electronic brochure, help leaflets and training seminars are available.

See also under: BRIGHTON: Sussex University Library.

Sussex University Library   ■

Address:	The University Library,
	University of Sussex,
	Falmer,
	Brighton,
	Sussex BN1 9QL
Tel:	01273 606755
Fax:	01273 678441

There are no substantial special collections of Middle Eastern material but the Library does have a quantity of relevant material covering history, Islam, politics etc. as part of its general stock.

Approximate numbers of books: Middle East history (including Israel) c.4000; Islam 500; Middle Eastern social conditions, politics, agriculture and industry etc. c.2000–3000; Arabic language and literature, fine art etc. c.300–400 vols.

Access: Any reader or researcher is permitted reference access to the collections.

See: MWP p. 228
See also under: BRIGHTON: British Library for Development Studies.

BRISTOL

■   Bristol University Library

Address:	University Library,
	University of Bristol,
	Tyndall Avenue,
	Bristol BS8 1TJ
Tel:	0117 928 8000
Fax:	0117 925 5334
Internet:	library@bris.ac.uk

Books on the Middle East form part of the general stock of the Library. They have been bought to support holdings in history, economics, sociology, politics, philosophy and religion. There is an undergraduate history option on the history of the Ottoman Empire.

Approximate numbers of books: History 1580; Islamic philosophy and religion 220; Arabic language and literature 80; Economics 125; Sociology 50; Politics 35; Islamic art 17.

Access: Access is to members of the University, and non-members on written application to the Librarian.

See: MWP p. 228, Pearson pp. 317–318, Roper 3 pp. 443–444.

BROMLEY

Bromley Central Library ■

Address:	Central Library,
	High Street,
	Bromley,
	Kent BR1 1EX
Tel:	0181 460 9955
Fax:	0181 313 9975

Bromley has acquired, as part of the subject specialisation scheme for the London and South Eastern Library Region (LASER), books listed in the BNB from January 1976 onwards in Dewey classes 915–919 and 950–999 (except children's books, school textbooks and very expensive items). This does not mean, however, that all other titles falling within these class bands are purchased for stock. Books collected thus include history and travel in the Middle East, although there is no separate Middle Eastern section. These books are part of the general library stock and mainly held in the Central Lending and Reference Libraries.

Approximate numbers of books: Middle East in general (Dewey nos. 915.6 & 956) 140 titles; Islam 50; Arab Gulf (history and travel) 30; Turkey (history and travel) 70; Egypt (history and travel) 125; Arabia (history and travel) 90; Iraq (history and travel) 65; Iran (history and travel) 90; Syria (history and travel) 25; Israel (history and travel) 325; Lebanon (history and travel) 20; Jordan (history and travel) 20.

Access: The Library is open to the general public.

CAMBRIDGE

■   Bible Society's Collections

Address: Bible Society's Librarian,
Cambridge University Library,
West Road,
Cambridge CB3 9DR
Tel: 01223 333000 ext. 3075
Fax: 01223 333160
e-mail: afj@ula.cam.ac.uk *or* rm@ula.cam.ac.uk

The Collections of the British and Foreign Bible Society have been housed at Cambridge University Library since 1984. They remain, however, the property of the Society. Materials are still being added; it is not a closed collection and enquiries are received and answered from all over the world. The collections include the *Scriptures Collection* comprising some 35,000 vols. in about 2200 languages including Arabic and thirteen dialects of Arabic; the *Manuscripts Collection* of some 500 items, 39 of which are in Arabic, including three Qur'ans; and the *Archives of the Society*, from its foundation in 1804, which include materials relating to the Middle East.

Access: The collections are open to bona fide researchers who can satisfy the entry criteria for the Cambridge University Library. For consulting the Archives it is essential to obtain prior permission from the Senior Information Officer/Archivist, British and Foreign Bible Society, Stonehill Green, Westlea, Swindon SN5 7DG (Tel: 01793 418100). A prior appointment is *essential* before coming to work at the University Library, and a letter of introduction should be provided for the first visit.

See: Pearson pp. 54, 93, 117, 145, 172, 314.

Cambridge University Library   ■

Address: Cambridge University Library,
West Road,
Cambridge CB3 9DR
Tel: 01223 333000
Fax: 01223 333160
e-mail: library@ula.cam.ac.uk *or* jb@ula.cam.ac.uk
URL: http://www.cam.ac.uk/libraries/

The Library's extensive general collections have from the beginning included works of Middle Eastern and Islamic interest (Averroes, Avicenna and Razi appear in a 1424 catalogue). Works in Arabic, Persian, Turkish and Hebrew appear in the general catalogues of the Library and for the most part stand as separately classified collections. The Library purchases regularly from a range of the Arab countries, and from Iran, Israel and Turkey. This material is richly reinforced by works in English and other Western languages, including early printed books (notable for early travel, among other subjects), maps, periodicals, official publications, and all the resources of a Copyright library augmented by a strong accessions policy. The Western material is largely organised on a subject, not an area, basis but a large part of the collection is open access and retrospective conversion of the catalogues is expanding the subject indexing which has been available for recent publications since 1978 in the computer catalogue (accessible via Telnet).

In a library of several million volumes it is not possible to quantify the substantial proportion relevant to Middle Eastern area studies.

It is worth stressing here that, as indicated above, the Library is entitled under the Copyright Act of 1911 to claim copies of all British publications.

In the manuscripts field, the Library has good holdings representing a full range of literature in Arabic (over 1500 vols.), Hebrew (over 1000 vols.), Persian (over 1200), Syriac (c.300), and Turkish (c.450), and E.G. Browne's collection of c.480 codices (Arabic, Persian and Turkish). It also holds major collections of documents, most notably the Cairo Genizah, over 140,000 fragments of documents and texts, principally in Hebrew and Judaeo-Arabic, providing a unique and outstanding resource for the study of the social, economic and religious life of the Near

Eastern Jewish communities of the 11th–13th centuries, with insights into their Arab milieu, and many aspects of earlier history, culture and literature.

The Michaelides Collection of some 2000 fragments (of which c.1000 Arabic and c.500 Coptic are on papyrus) covers an earlier period but extends as late as Ottoman Egypt. The papers of E.G. Browne contain an important archive of original and unique Persian material on the first constitutional period in Iran.

Most of the Islamic codices are described in the published catalogues, and many of the Genizah fragments in the thematic catalogues published in the Cambridge University Library's *Genizah Series*. The Hebrew manuscript catalogue is scheduled for publication in 1996; a computer catalogue of the Persian, Arabic and Turkish content of the Browne papers is being prepared for publication, as is a union catalogue of the Turkish manuscripts in Cambridge which is currently on fiche. Full details of the catalogues are available on request.

The Library also holds on deposit a collection of Islamic manuscripts belonging to Corpus Christi College and the two halves of the Pote Collection which are the property of King's College and Eton College respectively. Indo-Persian history and literature are well represented in all three. Papers of E.G. Browne which are the property of Pembroke College are housed alongside the Library's collection and included in the catalogue. The Collections of the Bible Society and of the Royal Commonwealth Society, which have separate entries in this Directory, are also now housed in the University Library.

Access: Access is principally for members of the University of Cambridge, but the Library is also used by the national and international academic community. Scholars and research students may be permitted to use the Library on production of letters of introduction: a modest charge may be made for such a ticket. Further details may be obtained from the Admissions Office within the Library.

See: Auch. pp. 30–33, Jones p. 218, MWP pp. 230–234, Pearson pp. 2, 56, 58, 91–92, 116, 172, 185–186, 303, 309–311, Roman pp. 34–38, Roper 3 pp. 445–451.
See also under: CAMBRIDGE: Bible Society's Collections
CAMBRIDGE: Royal Commonwealth Society Collections.
MASS: Arabian Peninsula.

Centre for Middle Eastern Studies   ■

See under: CAMBRIDGE: Faculty of Oriental Studies Library.

Centre of South Asian Studies Library   ■

Address:	Centre of South Asian Studies Library,
	Laundress Lane,
	Cambridge CB2 1SD
Tel:	01223 338094
Fax:	01223 316913
e-mail:	ljc10@cus.cam.ac.uk

The Centre was established in 1964 in accordance with the recommendations of the Hayter Report and was charged with promoting the study of South Asia in Cambridge. Since that time it has been actively collecting books in its subject areas – broadly, the social sciences, geography, history and, to a limited extent, religion, architecture, art and archaeology. In the late 1970s the Library extended its collecting policies to South East Asia and there is now a substantial collection for this region. The Library contains important holdings on Pakistan and Bangladesh, including the Islamic aspects of these States, and there is a small collection on Afghanistan. It holds general monographs on Islam and on the situation of Muslims in South and South East Asian countries. There is some material on the relationship of the Middle East with South and South East Asia. The Centre holds an archive of papers, photographs and cine films belonging to Europeans connected with South Asia.

Approximate size of holdings: The Centre now houses some 22,500 books; 3500 pamphlets; 4,000 vols. of serials; and 7500 microforms. The microforms include 2900 reels of South Asian newspapers as well as material copied from government archives. Necessarily only a small proportion of these holdings relate to the Middle East.

Access: Access is given to members of Cambridge University and to bona fide visiting scholars sponsored by persons of recognised academic standing. Use of the archival and microform collections is by appointment.

See: MWP pp. 234–235.

■ Christ's College Library

Address:	The Library, Christ's College, Cambridge CB2 3BU
Tel:	01223 334950
Fax:	01223 334904

The oriental collection (books and manuscripts) consists essentially of works given or bequeathed to the Library. Although a few modern works are purchased from time to time for undergraduate needs, it is not the policy of the College to compete with the Faculty of Oriental Studies Library (*qv*) or the Cambridge University Library (*qv*).

In 1821 Timothy Hutton presented to the College part of the library of his brother John, one of the Huttons of Marke in Yorkshire. The gift included oriental manuscripts (about 50 Persian and Turkish manuscripts). The other oriental manuscripts came from the collections of Sir Stephen Gaselee (Coptic) and W.H.D. Rouse (Indian). In 1894, under the will of Professor William Robertson Smith, the College received his large oriental library of printed books. Occasional purchases are still made for the Oriental Collection from the Robertson Smith Trust Fund. Dr. W.H.D. Rouse, who died in 1950, made many generous gifts to Christ's College Library including a collection of books on Indian Studies which contained many books in Sanskrit and Pali.

There is in the Library a catalogue of the oriental books but this is in need of revision. The whole of the Old Library in Christ's is at present being recatalogued and work has begun on the oriental section.

Approximate numbers of books: There are about 5000 printed books in the oriental collection in the following languages: Arabic, Persian, Hebrew, Syriac and Aramaic. There are several long runs of periodicals.

Approximate numbers of manuscripts: 58 oriental manuscripts in the Library have been described by Browne. There have also been some later additions. The manuscripts are in the following languages: Arabic, Aramaic, Persian, Coptic, Turkish, Sanskrit, Pali, Urdu and Chinese. There are about 70 altogether.

Access: The Bodley Library may be visited by all College members but the collections will be primarily of interest to visiting scholars who should make an appointment with the Librarian. The Arthur Peck Reading Room, the Law Library and the bookstacks are only open to members of the College.

See: Browne (Supp.) pp. 310–315 [Mss nos. 1348–1405], Munby pp. 2–4, Pearson pp. 92, 144–145, 310, Roman p. 38, Roper 3 pp. 451–452.

Corpus Christi College Library   ■

See under: CAMBRIDGE: Parker Library, Corpus Christi College.

East Asian History of Science Library   ■

Address: East Asian History of Science Library,
　　　　　　Needham Research Institute,
　　　　　　8, Sylvester Road,
　　　　　　Cambridge CB3 9AF
Tel:　　　01223 311545
Fax:　　　01223 62703
e-mail:　jm10019@cus.cam.ac.uk

The nucleus of this Library is material collected by Dr. Joseph Needham FRS FBA in the course of his research for *Science and Civilization in China* (CUP 1954–continuing). Dr. Needham's collection was taken over by a trust and, as a result of both gift and purchase, the Library now holds a good deal of material not directly related to Dr. Needham's work. The Islamic and Middle Eastern contribution to science and technology is represented in a very small way: there are about 100–200 books in European languages on Middle Eastern astronomy, medicine and alchemy.

Access: Readers have direct access to all books and periodicals but borrowing is not permitted.

Emmanuel College Library   ■

Address: The Library,
　　　　　　Emmanuel College,
　　　　　　Cambridge CB2 3AP
Tel:　　　01223 334233
Fax:　　　01223 334426

The Library contains a few texts, translations and reference books such as are needed by undergraduates reading Islamic and Middle Eastern subjects. There is also a small number of Islamic manuscripts.

Access: The Library is normally open only to members of the College. Visitors may be granted access by prior arrangement with the Librarian.

See: Munby pp. 12–13, Pearson pp. 59, 310, Roper 3 p. 453.

■   ## Faculty of Oriental Studies Library

Address:	Faculty of Oriental Studies Library,
	University of Cambridge,
	Sidgwick Avenue,
	Cambridge CB3 9DA
Tel:	01223 335111/2
Fax:	01223 335110
e-mail:	ors4@uk.ac.cam.ula

The Faculty collection is mainly concerned with language, literature, history, philosophy and religion of the Middle Eastern Islamic countries. It dates back to the 1930s and was formerly the library of the Oriental Institute, Cambridge. It contains many donations from the libraries of E.G. Browne, Reynold Nicholson, Reuben Levy and A.J. Arberry which include rare and valuable editions.

Approximate numbers of books: the collection of printed books and periodicals contains about 7000 vols. in all. The numbers of books in the main subject categories are as follows: Reference, dictionaries and grammars 1380 vols.; Geography and travel 360; History 840; Islam 1050; Art and Architecture 110; Philosophy and literature 2410; Others (Science, medicine etc.) 680; Arab Gulf (mainly historical works) 170.

The Library of the *Centre for Middle East Studies*, formerly a separate collection, is now also administered by the Faculty Library. It contains books concerning Turkey, Lebanon, Syria, Iraq, Iran, Jordan, Egypt and the countries of the Arabian Peninsula. Its subject area is mainly that of 19th and 20th century politics with special emphasis on the Gulf area and South Arabia.

Access: The Faculty of Oriental Studies Library is open to all members of the University and others on application to the Chairman of the Faculty Board. The catalogue (including holdings in Arabic) is available on-line in the Departmental file of the Cambridge University Library's catalogue which is accessible over the JANET network.

See: Roman p. 38, Roper 3 p. 445.
See also under: CAMBRIDGE: Queens' College Library.

King's College Library ■

See under: CAMBRIDGE: Cambridge University Library.

Middle East Centre Library ■

See under: CAMBRIDGE: Faculty of Oriental Studies Library.

Parker Library, Corpus Christi College ■

Address:	Parker Library, Corpus Christi College, Trumpington Street, Cambridge CB2 1RH
Tel:	01223 338025
Fax:	01223 338041

The Parker Library holds a collection of around 180 books, in the main donated to the College from the library of Henry Paine Stokes, Honorary Fellow 1912–1931, relating to the history of the Jewish people in England. All volumes must be consulted in the Parker Library.

Access: Applicants must apply in advance by letter, addressed to the Librarian, giving account of why they wish to visit the Library, of the volumes that they wish to see, and of their experience in handling early printed books. They must produce an academical letter of introduction from their home university or an institution of similar standing and documents of identification (e.g. passport or British Library reader's card).

See: Roman p. 38, Roper 3 pp. 452–453.
See also under: CAMBRIDGE: Cambridge University Library.

■ **Pembroke College Library**

Address: The Library,
Pembroke College,
Cambridge CB2 1RF
Tel: 01223 338121

Books have been acquired as required for undergraduate teaching. The Library contains about 100 general works on Arabic and Persian history, literature and criticism. It also has the Persian journals of E.G. Browne and the Papers of Sir Ronald Storrs.

Access: Access to the Library is confined to members of the College or other genuine visiting scholars, suitably accredited in advance. Only members of the College in residence may borrow books.

See: Jones p. 224, Munby pp. 32–33, MWP p. 240, Pearson pp. 59, 91, 310, Roper 3 pp. 456–457.
See also under: CAMBRIDGE: Cambridge University Library.

■ **Queens' College Library**

Address: The Library,
Queens' College,
Cambridge CB3 9ET
Tel: 01223 335549
Fax: 01223 335522
e-mail: que1@ula.cam.ac.uk

The oriental collection, which comprises about 355 volumes, is on long-term loan to the Faculty of Oriental Studies Library (*qv*). All items came to the college as a benefaction or purchases in the 19th Century.

Approximate numbers of books: Nearly all the works are in classical Arabic, but there are also 30 volumes of Turkish and 55 of Persian. Of the total number, about one third are dictionaries and grammars, one third Qur'ans and books on Islam and one third books on philosophy or literature.

In addition, the College has a small collection of oriental manuscripts which are still kept in the College itself. Eight of these are in Persian, several dating from the 16th Century, and one from the 14th. There are also 5 Turkish manuscripts, mainly dating from the 17th Century.

Access: Applications to consult the manuscripts should be made to the Librarian of Queens' College. The oriental collection is a closed private collection. Scholars may have access on application to the Librarian of Queens' College or to the Librarian of the Faculty of Oriental Studies Library. A project is on hand to add the catalogue to Cambridge University Departmental and Colleges Union Catalogue which is accessible via JANET.

See: Browne (Supp.) p. 307, Munby pp. 36–37, Pearson p. 310, Roper 3 p. 457.

Royal Commonwealth Society Collections   ■

Address:	Royal Commonwealth Society Collections,
	Cambridge University Library,
	West Road,
	Cambridge CB3 9DR
Tel:	01223 333198
Fax:	01223 333160
e-mail:	tab@ula.cam.ac.uk

The Royal Commonwealth Society (RCS) was founded as the Colonial Society in 1868 and built up its library from that date, though it contains some books published before its foundation. The main concern has always been the countries of the Empire and Commonwealth but it has also collected material in areas of British influence and hence possesses substantial material on Egypt (particularly during the period of the British Protectorate), the Sudan and the Asian countries of the Middle East, particularly those which have been British mandates. There is also a substantial pamphlet collection, together with a collection of official publications, manuscripts and a photograph collection which includes 19th and early 20th century photographs of Palestine and Egypt.

The RCS Library was transferred from London to Cambridge University Library in the summer of 1993 after a successful appeal for £3m prevented sale and dispersal. A project is now underway to add its records to the main Cambridge University Library Catalogue.

Approximate numbers of books: (Bound books only): Asian countries of the Middle East (viz Aden, Arabia, Jordan, Israel, Iraq, Iran, The Gulf) 1000; Egypt 500; Sudan 300; Francophone North Africa 200; Libya 30; Islam in general 50; Islam in Africa 50; Cyprus 600. There are also books on Asia and Africa generally, on French and Italian colonisation, on Pakistan and the political history of the Indian sub-continent and on Northern Nigeria, which would include substantial relevant material not represented in the above figures.

Access: Those wishing to consult the RCS Collections must go through the usual University Library admissions procedure. It is advisable (but not essential) to contact the RCS Collections Librarian in advance of the first visit.

See: Jones pp. 163, 225, MWP pp. 189–190.

See also: Evans Lewin, *The Subject Catalogue of the Royal Empire Society* (4 vols.); Royal Commonwealth Society, *The Biography Catalogue*; Royal Commonwealth Society, *The Subject Catalogue of the Royal Commonwealth Society* (7 vols. with 2 supp. vols.); Donald H. Simpson (ed.), *The Manuscript Catalogue of the Royal Commonwealth Society*. For an account of the development of the collections up to the transfer to Cambridge, see Terry A. Barringer, 'The Rise, Fall and Rising Again of the Royal Commonwealth Society Library', *African Research and Documentation*.

■ St. Catherine's College Library

Address:	The Library,
	St. Catherine's College,
	Cambridge CB2 1RL
Tel:	01223 338343
Fax:	01223 338340
e-mail:	cthl@ula.cam.ac.uk

There is no Islamic and Middle East collection as such, although dictionaries, literature and history books have been acquired as required for undergraduate teaching and are listed in the Cambridge University Union Catalogue. However, the Library holds a collection of Bibles, grammars and dictionaries in many European and Eastern languages formed by Thomas Jarrett (1805–1882) who was at different periods of his career Professor of Arabic and Regius

Professor of Hebrew at Cambridge University. Some of the collection has been dispersed but the bulk remains. Many of the volumes are in a frail condition. Approximate numbers of books: The catalogue for the Jarrett Collection is handwritten and unreliable and it has been impossible to estimate the percentage of the Collection directly relevant to this Directory.

Access: Access is restricted to members of the College and to visiting scholars by appointment.

See: Munby pp. 39–40, Pearson p. 310, Roper 3 p. 457.

St. John's College Library ■

Address:	The Library,
	St. John's College,
	Cambridge CB2 1TP
Tel:	01223 338662 (general)
	01223 339393 (manuscripts)

The Library contains a few modern textbooks. There are also about 40 Arabic manuscripts.

Access: Visiting scholars by appointment.

See: Browne (Supp.) pp. 315–319 [Mss nos. 1406–1444], Munby pp. 41–43, MWP p. 240, Pearson pp. 59, 310, Roman p. 38, Roper 3 p. 458.

Trinity College Library ■

Address:	The Library,
	Trinity College,
	Cambridge CB2 1TQ
Tel:	01223 338488
Fax:	01223 338532

The College has an important collection of Islamic and Middle Eastern manuscripts. There is, however, no collection of secondary material relating to these manuscripts. The Library has the papers of Professor J. Palmer (1769–1840).

Access: Readers are admitted by appointment.

See: Munby pp. 46–50, MWP p. 240, Pearson pp. 56, 58, 92, 310, Roman p. 38, Roper 3 p. 458.

See also: E.H. Palmer, *A Descriptive Catalogue of the Arabic, Persian and Turkish Manuscripts in the Library of Trinity College, Cambridge*; H. Loewe, *Catalogue of the Manuscripts in the Hebrew Character Collected and Bequeathed to Trinity College Library by the late William Aldis Wright.*

■ ## Westminster College Library

Address:	The Library,
	Westminster College,
	Madingley Road,
	Cambridge CB3 0AA
Tel:	01223 359247

The Library has collections on Judaism and the Old Testament but the collection of greatest significance is the Lewis-Gibson Collection of manuscript fragments from the Cairo Genizah, bought by Mrs. Agnes Smith Lewis and Mrs. Margaret Dunlop Gibson at the time of the opening of the Genizah and presented to the College soon after its move to Cambridge in 1899.

Approximate numbers of books: Books on Judaism 550; Books on Old Testament 1800; Manuscript fragments in Hebrew and Judaeo-Arabic from the Cairo Genizah 1500.

Access: The Genizah Collection is always under lock and key, and it is necessary to make an appointment with the Honorary Librarian to have access to it.

See: Munby p. 56, Pearson pp. 58, 92, 310.

CANTERBURY

Kent University Library   ■

See under: CANTERBURY: Templeman Library, University of Kent.

Templeman Library, University of Kent   ■

Address:	The Templeman Library,
	University of Kent,
	Canterbury,
	Kent CT2 7NU
Tel:	01227 764000
Fax:	01227 475495
e-mail:	library @ukc.ac.uk

The Library holds some 600 volumes on Islam, including Islamic Law. They are used particularly to support an MA in Islamic Studies. There are seven current serials in this field. The Library possesses a strong Biblical Studies collection and a number of works on Judaism and Jewish history. Religious and Theological Abstracts is available on CD-ROM.

Access: Non-members of the University should apply to the Librarian in the first instance.

COVENTRY

■   BP Archive, University of Warwick

Address: BP Archive,
           The Library,
           University of Warwick,
           Coventry CV4 7AL
Tel: 01203 524517
Fax: 01203 524523

The Archive is to be found in the new library extension which is next to the central University Library. The main collection of the Archive comprises roughly 9500 linear feet of records covering the history of the BP group from 1901 to the present day. Material pre-dating 1954 is available to bona fide researchers in the public search room. It is intended that further material will be opened in the future. The usual core business records are to be found, such as annual reports and accounts, minutes of board meetings, memoranda and articles of association and so forth. However, more detail of the Company's operations can usually be found in the reports and working papers which together make up roughly half the collection. Numerous photographs are also available. Company magazines and public relations material can prove interesting, and the current 1954 cut-off date does not apply to them.

Included in the above collection are the records of the Kuwait Oil Company. The BP Archive also acts as custodian for archives of the Iranian Oil Participants and the Iraq Petroleum Company. This material is currently closed to the public, though access to the latter is sometimes granted by permission of the owners.

Access: Use of the Archives is by prior appointment and may be arranged by letter addressed to the Senior Archivist. See also the note on access to certain archives, immediately above. A leaflet describing the BP Archive is available (from the address at the top of this entry), entitled 'BP Archive: An Introduction for Readers'.

APPENDIX: A Brief History of BP: The following brief history of BP, supplied by the Archive, illustrates the Middle Eastern connections of BP and highlights the importance of the BP Archive at the University of Warwick for Middle East researchers.

The Company was incorporated in 1909 as the Anglo-Persian Oil Company to exploit the discovery of oil in commercial quantities in Persia in 1908. Its first refinery was commissioned at Abadan, Persia, in 1913. In 1914 the British Government invested £2 million in the Company, replacing the Burmah Oil Company as the major shareholder. The Company formed the British Tanker Company in 1915, and after World War I extended its international oil exploration, refining and marketing activities. In 1928 and 1932 joint marketing companies were formed with Shell, covering the 'consolidated area' (Southern and Eastern Africa, parts of the Levant and the Western and Southern littoral of Arabia) and the UK. During the 1920s and 1930s the Company was engaged in exploration across the world, but its strength continued to rest on huge reserves in the Middle East. The Company held an interest in the Iraq Petroleum Company which had been set up to exploit the potential oil reserves of the old Ottoman empire and which came to hold extensive oil exploration rights in Iraq, the Levant and the Trucial Coast. Oil was discovered in Iraq in 1927. The Company, renamed the Anglo-Iranian Oil Company in 1935, was also a partner in the Kuwait Oil Company which discovered oil at Burgan in 1938.

A new concession agreed between the Persian Government and the Company in 1933 reduced the area available for exploration and changed the way in which royalties were calculated. However, further disagreements about the terms of the concession resulted in a major crisis for the Company when its assets in Iran (as Persia was now called) were nationalised by the Iranian Government in 1951. In an attempt to compensate for this loss of nearly three quarters of its production and refining capacity, Anglo-Iranian increased output from Iraq and Kuwait; and international exploration was intensified, soon yielding substantial finds in Abu Dhabi. After three years of negotiations the Company formed part (40 per cent) of a consortium of oil companies, the Iranian Oil Participants, which re-entered the Iranian Oil Industry in 1954. In December of that year the Company was renamed British Petroleum (BP).

More recently BP has expanded its involvement in petrochemicals, taking over the chemical interests of Distillers Company in 1967. Following a major oil discovery in Alaska in 1969, it merged its main US interests with those of Standard Oil (Ohio), of which it gained full ownership in 1987. The Company discovered the large Forties oil field in the North Sea in 1970, but lost direct access to most of its supplies of OPEC oil as a result of the OPEC crises of the 1970s. Since the early 1970s BP's focus has moved away from the Middle East where its origins were laid; but after a period of increased diversification, during which the Company expanded its interests in computer software, nutrition, coal and minerals, it is now concentrating once again on its core hydro-carbon based activities.

■ Modern Records Centre, University of Warwick

Address:	Modern Records Centre,
	University Library,
	University of Warwick,
	Coventry CV4 7AL
Tel:	01203 523523/524219
Fax:	01203 524211
e-mail:	lycw@libris.lib.warwick.ac.uk

In the Modern Records Centre Information Leaflet No.1 entitled 'Notes for Researchers', the Centre states that it 'aims to collect and make available for research original sources for British political, social and economic history, with particular reference to labour history, industrial relations and industrial politics.' The leaflet continues: 'The type of material held by the Centre includes signed minutes, correspondence files, runs of printed journals and ephemera of trade unions, the TUC registry files pre-1960, and records of employers' and trade associations, including the CBI and its predecessors. It also holds records of some interest groups and political organisations (including West Midlands), of individuals and business (particularly the motor industry). The Library's 41T&U series, including the Board of Trade Library collection, may also be consulted in the Centre.'

The Centre contains important Jewish and Middle East related material in a number of the principal accessions, notably FBI (Federation of British Industries) Files, the Gollancz Papers, the Eichmann files, Standard Motor Company Files, TUC Files and the Papers of Richard Crossman (1907–1974). Much fuller details of all this material will be found in APPENDIX TWO of this Directory.

Access: All material is kept in closed accommodation and may be worked on only in the Centre, under the supervision of its staff. Some deposits are subject to restriction on their use for research.

Warwick University Library ∎

Address: The Library,
University of Warwick,
Coventry CV4 7AL
Tel: 01203 524103

The University has no courses specifically relating to Middle Eastern Studies and the collection is therefore limited to such books as are relevant to other subject areas. There is a particularly strong collection of Jewish history books, and there is also a sizeable Statistics collection.

Approximate numbers of books: There is a total of c.5000 monograph volumes covering Islam, Judaism and the Middle East: Islam (Religion and Philosophy) c.300 vols.; Judaism (Religion) c.300 vols.; Middle Eastern history c.1000 vols.; Jewish history c.1700 vols.; Other Arts c.100 vols.; Politics c.500 vols.; Sociology c.200 vols.; Economics c.100 vols.; Law c.100 vols.; Statistics c.700 titles (current c.90 vols.); Periodicals c.40 titles (current c.30 titles).

Access: Access to the Library is restricted to card-holders only. Applications for reference use should be made in writing to the Librarian. There is no one librarian responsible for all Middle Eastern books. Enquiries should therefore be made, in the first instance, to the General Enquiries desk which is on the first floor of the Library.

DUBLIN

■ **Archbishop Marsh's Library**

Address:	Archbishop Marsh's Library,
	St. Patrick's Close,
	Dublin 8, Eire
Tel:	003531 4543511
Fax:	003531 4543511

Archbishop Marsh's Library has the distinction of being the first public library in Ireland. It was built in 1701 and contains about 25,000 books dating from 1472–1750. Marsh left a large collection of oriental manuscripts to the Bodleian Library, Oxford (*qv*) but he left all his books to his own library. Among these are books in Arabic, Hebrew, Syriac, Armenian, Coptic, Ethiopic, Georgian, Persian and Turkish. There are beautiful editions of the Talmud and Targums as well as a missal in Arabic and the epitome of Baronius' *Annals* in Arabic from 1653.

Access: Marsh's Library is still a public library and was intended by Marsh to remain a public library forever. It was never a lending library. Because of the nature of the collections, the majority of the users today tend to be scholars and undergraduate and postgraduate students from the universities.

See: MWP p. 385.
See also: G.T. Stokes, *Some Worthies of the Irish Church*, ed. by H.J. Lawlor, pp. 72–74; Muriel McCarthy, *All Graduates and Gentlemen: Marsh's Library*, pp. 165–166.

■ **Chester Beatty Library**

Address:	The Chester Beatty Library,
	20, Shrewsbury Road,
	Dublin 4, Eire.
	[NB The Library will move to The Clock Tower Building,
	Dublin Castle, in 1997]
Tel:	003531 2692386
Fax:	003531 2830983

Sir Alfred Chester Beatty (1875–1968) was born in New York but had two Irish grandparents. He was both a mining engineer and an art collector and his superb Qur'an collection may have been fostered by the beautiful Qur'ans which he encountered in Cairo in the early part of this century. Beatty moved to Dublin in 1950 and built a special library in Shrewsbury Road to hold his books and manuscripts. His collection was left in trust to the people of Ireland and comprises c.13,000 volumes and other objects.

The Library contains a reference section of books with holdings on Islamic and Mughal Art. However, the main Islamic collection consists of 3000 Arabic manuscripts on diverse topics, collected to show the breadth of Islamic Culture. There are 300 Persian, 250 Turkish and 70 Mughal manuscripts, collected mainly for their artistic value. The Library's very important Qur'an collection consists of some 300 manuscripts from every part of the Islamic world.

Access: Access is for accredited scholars on application to the Director.

See: Pearson pp. 83, 110, 126, 138–139, 164, 246–248, Roman pp. 50–52, Roper 2 pp. 53–61, Roper 4 pp. 261–262.

See also: A.J. Arberry, *The Chester Beatty Library: A Handlist of the Arabic Manuscripts* (8 vols.); idem., *The Koran Illuminated*; A.J. Arberry, M. Minovi & E. Blochet, *The Chester Beatty Library: A Catalogue of the Persian Manuscripts and Miniatures*; David James, *Qur'ans and Bindings from the Chester Beatty Library: A Facsimile Exhibition*; B.P. Kennedy, *Alfred Chester Beatty and Ireland 1950–1968: A Study in Cultural Politics*; Linda Leach, *Mughal and Other Indian Paintings from the Chester Beatty Library*; V. Minorsky, *The Chester Beatty Library: A Catalogue of the Turkish Manuscripts and Miniatures*.

National Library of Ireland   ■

Address:	National Library of Ireland,
	Kildare Street,
	Dublin 2, Eire
Tel:	003531 6618811
Fax:	003531 6766690

Since the National Library of Ireland is primarily a library of Irish Studies, there is little in the collections concerning the Middle East, with the exception of copies of some 18th and 19th century travel books, most of which would not be uncommon. However, the Library does have a small number of manuscripts, including Qur'ans.

Access: Applications to read in the National Library should be made in person during opening hours. Applicants must produce identification (e.g. passport). A separate application should be made to consult manuscripts. The National Library is closed for the Calendar month of *December* each year to allow for checking of stock.

See: Department of Education, *Report of the Council of Trustees of the National Library of Ireland for 1977* for a listing of the manuscripts.

■ Royal Irish Academy Library

Address:	Royal Irish Academy Library,
	19, Dawson Street,
	Dublin 2, Eire
Tel:	003531 6762570/6764222
Fax:	003531 6762346

The Library contains a very few diverse oriental manuscripts and drawings relating to the East which include fragments of a Hebrew Pentateuchal scroll, and Arabic and Persian manuscripts.

Access: Access to the collections is available to research scholars on recommendation of members, or with an introduction from a faculty or other library. An annual fee is payable.

See: Roper 2 p. 61.

■ Trinity College Library

Address:	Trinity College Library,
	University of Dublin,
	College Street,
	Dublin 2, Eire
Tel:	003531 6772941
Fax:	003531 6719003
Telex:	003531 25442
e-mail:	bmeehan@tcd.ie (manuscripts)
	emcglade@tcd.ie (readers' services)

As a British and Irish copyright library since 1801, Trinity College Library receives books and periodicals dealing with the Middle East, but this is not a major subject area taught in Trinity and so the collection has not been extensively developed.

Approximate numbers of books and periodicals: There are approximately 600 volumes of books and 400 volumes of periodicals on open-access shelves, dealing with Judaism, Arabic, the history of pre-Christian Bible lands etc. There are other items on these subjects, received under the Copyright Act, in the closed stacks but it is not possible to estimate the numbers involved.

Approximate number of manuscripts: There are 200 oriental manuscripts.

Access: Access is available to members of the College. Others wishing to use the Library should make advance application in writing to the Librarian, giving details of the items they wish to consult.

See: MWP pp. 385–386, Pearson pp. 83, 110, 139, 248, 303, Roman p. 52, Roper 2 pp. 62–64, Roper 4 p. 262.
See also: T.K. Abbott, *Catalogue of the Manuscripts in the Library of Trinity College, Dublin.*

DURHAM

■ Documentation Unit of the Centre for Middle Eastern and Islamic Studies

See under: DURHAM: Durham University Library.

■ Durham University Library

Address:	The University Library, University of Durham, Stockton Road, Durham DH1 3LY
Tel:	0191 374 3018
Fax:	0191 374 7481
Telex:	317210 BT Bureau Service
e-mail:	main.library@durham.ac.uk

Durham University Library has wide-ranging collections covering the Middle Eastern and Islamic World, which have been built up, largely since 1950, in support of the University's teaching and research programmes. These are currently (1995) divided between two sites, the **Main Library** at Stockton Road which houses the **main loan** and **reference** collection of books, journals, pamphlets and newspapers together with the **Middle East Documentation Unit (MEDU)** (transferred from the Centre for Middle Eastern and Islamic Studies in 1993), and the **Palace Green Section**, where relevant **early printed books, manuscripts**, and **archival material** are housed.

Main Loan and Reference Collection: This collection covers all Middle Eastern and North African countries from ancient to modern times, including Iran and Turkey, and extends to Ethiopia, Afghanistan, the Caucasus and the Central Asian Republics. There are substantial amounts of material in Arabic, Persian and Turkish. There is a large section on Islam, which is covered worldwide. There is a comprehensive journal collection and the Library subscribes to six current daily newspapers from the Middle East; back issues of these and other older titles are retained in the Library Store. Under the MELCOM Specialisation Scheme Durham has responsibility for the Sudan and aims at as comprehensive a coverage of printed materials relating to the Sudan as possible.

The Middle East Documentation Unit: MEDU was set up in 1970 as a collection of primary documents on the political, social and economic development of the modern Middle East and now contains over 200,000 items. The Unit covers all Arab countries, Iran, Israel and Turkey, with smaller collections on Afghanistan, Central Asia, Cyprus, the Horn of Africa, Malta and Pakistan. Coverage generally starts in the 1960s but in some cases from 1945. Types of documents held include selected publications of Middle Eastern governments, agencies and regional organisations, a wide range of news journals and newsletters relating to the region, annual reports and journals of Middle Eastern banks, oil companies and other industries, transport organisations and educational establishments, political parties and pressure groups, along with selected publications of international organisations working in the region.

Early Printed Books, Archives and Manuscripts: These comprise a significant resource for research on the Middle East and Islam. The early printed books include material published up to 1850 together with valuable material of later date. Archival and manuscript collections of Middle Eastern interest include the Sudan Archive which focuses on the Anglo-Egyptian Condominium 1899–1955, and is backed up by a sizeable related special collection of printed material, the **Abbas Hilmi 11 Papers**, the **T.M. Johnstone Papers** on modern South Arabian languages, and a small Islamic manuscripts collection.

Access (including Catalogue access): The Library is open to all members of the University and to other persons on written application to the Librarian. Prior contact in advance of a visit is advised.

External access to Library catalogues is as follows:

The URL for the OPAC is: telnet://progate.dur.ac.uk.600
The URL for the MEDU
catalogue (MEDUSA) is: telnet://melib.dur.ac.uk
                                              login and password melib

Records for the early printed books are gradually being added to the OPAC. Conversion of finding aids for achival and manuscript collections to machine-readable form is underway and these are expected to be accessible through the World Wide Web in 1996. Summary guides to the Sudan Archive and the Abbas Hilmi 11 Papers are available and Volume 1 of the Catalogue of the Papers of General Sir Reginald Wingate (1861–1953) held in the Sudan Archive were scheduled for publication in 1996.

See: Auch. pp. 34–42, Jones p. 218, MWP pp. 251–265, Pearson pp. 60, 318, Roman pp. 43–44, Roper 3 458–460.
See also: M.W. Daly & L.E. Forbes, *The Sudan: Caught in Time.*

MASS: Sudan.

■   Durham University Oriental Museum

Address: The Oriental Museum,
           Elvet Hill,
           Durham DH1 3TH
Tel: 0191 374 2911
Fax: 0191 374 3242
e-mail: oriental.museum@durham.ac.uk

This is the only museum in the UK devoted exclusively to Oriental art and antiquities. The area of interest ranges from the Maghrib to Japan and from prehistoric to modern times. The Museum is included in this Directory as a further illustration of the University of Durham's activities in the Middle Eastern and Oriental field.

The Museum was founded on the collection of Egyptian antiquities formed by the 4th Duke of Northumberland in the mid-19th Century and acquired by the University in 1950. The collection is a fine general collection but concentrates on small objects of high quality including statuary, stone vessels and amulets and jewellery in faience, glass and metal. There is also a comprehensive collection of funerary stelai. The collection has been considerably enlarged since 1950 by the addition of many similar items and was arranged in a completely new display in 1993.

The ancient Near East is represented by excavated material from Jerusalem, Jericho, Lachish, Ur and Nimrud and by other items of unknown provenance, including two reliefs, probably from Nineveh and a large collection of seals. From the modern Near East there are Palestinian textiles and ethnographic items from the Tihama.

There is a small collection of Islamic art, mostly ceramics but with some metalwork and a few examples of fine calligraphy and miniatures. Several of the miniatures and metalwork items are of Mughal origin, as are a number of fine quality jades.

Other major Oriental cultures are well represented in the Museum: China in particular by a wide range of artefacts, Japan mainly by prints and *inros*, Tibet by *thangkas* and India by Gandhara sculptures. The diversity allows for cross-cultural displays such as those on Eastern Religions, the Silk Road and the Development of Writing.

Access: Although based in a university, the displays are arranged with the needs of the general public in mind. Areas of the collection are currently being recorded on a database with a view to making handlists readily available. Enquiries from researchers are welcome.

EDINBURGH

■ ## Edinburgh University Library

Address:	Edinburgh University Library,
	George Square,
	Edinburgh EH8 9LJ
Tel:	0131 650 3384
Fax:	0131 667 9780
Telex:	727442 (UNIVED G)
e-mail:	library@edinburgh.ac.uk

The growth of the Islamic and Middle Eastern collections in Edinburgh University Library has followed and reflected the needs of the teaching programme, as well as the research interests of the staff and students. Primary research areas are Islam (worldwide), history, law, language and literature. Arabic has been taught as an independent subject at Edinburgh University since 1912, with Persian, Turkish and a degree course in Islamic history being introduced in the 1940s. The Library's collections in Arabic are stronger than those in Persian and Turkish. The collections are housed principally in the Main Library, George Square, where they are dispersed according to subject. There is an Islamic class library within the Muir Institute (7–8 Buccleuch Place) which contains a significant proportion of books not held in the Main Library, and New College Library at Mound Place, the library of the Faculty of Divinity, also houses older material in Middle Eastern languages. This includes some 430 books from the library of the Hon. Ion Keith-Falconer (1856–1887).

The Special Collections Department in the Main Library holds a collection of over 650 items of Middle Eastern interest, mainly in Arabic and Persian, but with some Turkish, and is notable for the 14th Century manuscript of Rashid al-Din's *Jam' al-Tawarikh* which forms a major surviving example of early Persian painting.

A recent acquisition, still being catalogued, is the library of the late Professor R.B. Serjeant (1915–1993) which is rich in books on the Yemen; enquiries should be made to the Special Collections Librarian (Tel: 0131 650 3412).

A good general selection of CD-ROMs is available.

Access: Applications for admission to the Main Library and/or to the Islamic Class Library should be made in writing to the University Librarian.

See: Auch. pp. 78–80, MWP pp. 353–354, 360, Pearson pp. 61, 93, 118, 173, 319, Roman pp. 45–47. Roper 3 pp. 460–463.
See also: M.A. Hukk, H. Ethé & E. Robertson, *A Descriptive Catalogue of the Arabic and Persian Manuscripts in the Edinburgh University Library*; Edinburgh University Library, *Oriental Manuscripts: A Continuation of the Descriptive Catalogue of 1925, By Hukk, Ethé & Robertson* (Handlist H9, 1994).

National Library of Scotland   ■

Address:	National Library of Scotland,
	George IV Bridge,
	Edinburgh EH1 1EW
Tel:	0131 226 4531
Fax:	0131 220 6662

The Library has very little printed material in Arabic or any other Middle Eastern language since it has never attempted to collect it. It is a British library of legal deposit, however, and has, therefore, an extensive collection of *British* publications relating to Islam and the Middle East, especially publications of the 20th Century. There are a few manuscripts in Arabic and Persian. The Library also has an extensive (general) map collection, which covers the Middle Eastern area with sheet maps pretty well, insofar as they exist or are available. Lebanon, Turkey and modern Israel are covered by 1:100,000 and 1:250,000 scale maps; Iran by 1:1,000,000 and 1:500,000. A series of War Office maps, not complete, is available for Iraq, Yemen etc. The *Tübingen Atlas des Vorderen Orients* is taken.

Access: The Reading Rooms may be used for research that cannot readily be done elsewhere. Admission is by a 3-year reader's ticket or a short-term ticket.

See: Jones p. 223, MWP pp. 354–360, Pearson pp. 61, 92, 118, 320, Roman p. 47, Roper 3 pp. 463–464.
See also under: EDINBURGH: National Register of Archives (Scotland).

■ National Register of Archives (Scotland)

Address: National Register of Archives (Scotland),
HM General Register House,
2, Princes Street,
Edinburgh EH1 3YY
Tel: 0131 535 1405/1403
Fax: 0131 535 1430

The National Register of Archives (Scotland) (NRA (S)) was set up by the Scottish Record Office in 1946 to compile a record of collections of private papers in Scotland. Almost 4000 lists or 'surveys' have now been added to the Register and these are available for consultation by researchers in the search rooms of the Scottish Record Office (*qv*) and the National Library of Scotland in Edinburgh (*qv*) and the Royal Commission on Historical Manuscripts in London. The lists describe papers held by private individuals and families, landed estates, clubs and societies, businesses and law firms. The Register also includes lists of similar papers which have been deposited with the archives and libraries of local authorities, universities, institutions and companies. Source lists covering the first 1000 surveys are available for the Middle East (No. 20), Africa (No. 21), India and the Far East (No. 22), Europe (No. 25) and also for travel diaries and letters (No. 26). Existing surveys are gradually being transferred to a computerised Register, which will facilitate searches by readers in the Scottish Record Office.

Access: While the staff of the NRA(S) are always pleased to answer limited and specific postal enquiries concerning the existence of papers relating to a particular subject or individual, they are unable to undertake research on behalf of enquirers.

See: Jones p. 223.

Scottish Record Office   ▪

Address:	Scottish Record Office,
	HM General Register House,
	Edinburgh
	EH1 3YY
Tel:	0131 535 1333/1413 (Search Rooms)
Fax:	0131 535 1360

There are substantial collections of muniments and records relating to the Middle East, and to Islam elsewhere, held by the Scottish Record Office (SRO). The SRO took considerable trouble to make an identification of all the main relevant collections and full details are therefore listed in APPENDIX THREE of this volume.

Access: Access to collections is unrestricted with the exception of a few deposited collections (GDs) for which a 'Restricted Access' form must be signed beforehand, agreeing to consultation with the owners before publication. Large-scale copying of many collections is also restricted in this way.

See: Jones p. 225, MWP pp. 360–370.
See also: Two very useful leaflets which are available for researchers: (i) *Facilities for Historical Research* (SRO Leaflet No.5) and (ii) *Scottish Record Office: Preserving and Providing Access to our National Archival Heritage*. A selection of other free information leaflets, including one entitled *How to Use the Record Office*, is available on request.
See also under: EDINBURGH: National Register of Archives (Scotland)

EGHAM

■ Royal Holloway College Library

Address:	Royal Holloway College Library,
	University of London,
	Egham Hill,
	Egham,
	Surrey TW20 0EX
Tel:	01784 443334
Fax:	01784 477670
Telex:	935504 RHCLIB

The Library has about 2000 items on the Middle East, covering its history – economic, political and social – geography and geology as well as some basic books in Hebrew and Arabic.

Access: There is no charge for members of the general public who wish to make use of the Library purely for self-service reference purposes. Borrowing privileges attract an annual charge. This charge allows readers to borrow seven items from the stock on open access with the exception of items in the Restricted Loans Collection and items confined to the Library such as journals.

EXETER

Documentation Unit, Centre for Arab Gulf Studies   ■

Address:	Documentation Unit,
	Centre for Arab Gulf Studies,
	University of Exeter,
	Old Library,
	Prince of Wales Road,
	Exeter,
	Devon EX4 4JZ
Tel:	01392 264041
Fax:	01392 264023
e-mail:	p.foroughi@uk.ac.ex.cen
WWW:	http:www.ex.ac.uk/~ajrathme/docintro.htm

The Documentation Unit of the Centre for Arab Gulf Studies was set up in 1980 to collect a very wide range of basic documentation on all aspects of the region: economics, politics, development, social and cultural aspects and history. The region covered consists primarily of the countries of the Arab Gulf and the Arabian Peninsula. The collection of current documentation for this area is very comprehensive, from about mid-century, with some titles going back to early this century. Important titles are continuously updated and every effort is made to collect back issues, sometimes on microfiche. Considerable documentation is also kept for the wider region from Egypt and the Levant through to Iran, but in this wider region there is only an active acquisitions policy for Palestine.

The holdings, including grey materials and unpublished items, are impossible to quantify in terms of volumes, but they currently occupy over 1000 metres of shelving in the Unit itself, with more in store elsewhere. Material ranges from official reports, statistics, development plans, press releases and periodicals, etc., from Arab Gulf government departments, financial institutions, commerce and industry to reports on Gulf countries from international and regional organisations and foreign sources. There is also a uniquely comprehensive collection of Arab Gulf newspapers and many other periodicals. In addition to current documentation the Unit specialises in history and archival material from the mid-16th

Century, with a particular strength in Arab Gulf History from 1780 onward. The selected extracts from the *Bombay Diaries: Secret and Political Department Series* (16,000 photocopied pages from 1778 to 1820, with typescripts and guide), are a unique resource not otherwise available except in Bombay. There are also collections of relevant microfilms from British and American, Indian, French and Portuguese government archives, and all the relevant publications by *Archive Editions*, 45 titles, currently about 450 volumes. Several collections of private papers and diaries are also held. The Unit's holdings range widely and cover general Middle East studies, especially economics, with a particular strength in finance and petroleum in which there are many considerable and continuing runs of official reports and periodical titles. There is media coverage in the form of cuttings collections from the world press, including a classified microfiche collection from 1956 to 1982; and media surveys, viz. the *BBC Summary of World Broadcasts* from 1955 onwards, and *Mid-East Mirror* (English translation of extracts from the Arabic Press), complete from its first issue in 1987, both title runs complete and continuing.

There is also extensive documentation and archival material on the subject of Palestine, as well as a considerable holding of monographs and periodicals. The Palestine Studies Trust has donated considerable funds for microfilms from the American and British Archives and records of UN activities.

Important additions to the collection in 1994–1995 included:

– *Ya'akov Firestone Collection*: Documentation on the history and demography of the Palestinian village of Arrabeh from the late 19th Century to 1970.
– The Archive of the *Gulf Information Project*, set up in 1991 to monitor the effects of the Iraq–Kuwait War, including international reports and documents, press cuttings, files etc.
– The Library of the London Office of *Petronal*: this substantially enhances and extends the collection on Middle East economics and petroleum.

Access (including Catalogue access): Access is freely available to any student or researcher, for reference only. There are facilities for photocopying. The Catalogues listing the main holdings of the Unit are now available on the World Wide Web, and a project for more detailed on-line cataloguing of the holdings has begun.

See: Auch. p. 46.

MASS: Arabian Peninsula [Exeter does not collect extensively vernacular periodicals or works of literature]; Iraq [Monographs only].

Exeter University Library ∎

Address:	Exeter University Library,
	Stocker Road,
	Exeter,
	Devon EX4 4PT
	Main Middle Eastern collections are held in:
	Old Library,
	University of Exeter,
	Prince of Wales Road,
	Exeter,
	Devon EX4 4PT
Tel:	01392 263873 (Main Library)
	01392 264052 (Old Library)
	01392 264051 (Old Library – Subject Specialist)
Fax:	01392 263871
e-mail:	j.p.c.auchterlonie@exeter.ac.uk
URL:	http://www.ex.ac.uj/~ijtilsed/lib/libintro.html

The University Library has been collecting material in the field of Arabic, Islamic and Middle Eastern Studies since 1973, to support taught courses and research principally within the Department of Arabic and Middle East Studies, the Department of Politics, the Department of Spanish, the Centre for Arab Gulf Studies and the Centre for Mediterranean Studies. The Middle Eastern Collections within the Library now total around 24,000 volumes, about half of which are in Arabic. Most of this material is housed in the Arabic Collection in the Old Library (where the Subject Specialist Librarian is based), but there are important holdings in the politics and history of the Middle East and in Hispano-Arabic Studies in the Main Library as well.

The collections are strong in the fields of classical Arabic and Islamic culture, particularly history, Arabic language and literature, and Hispano-Arabic Studies. Modern Arabic literature, and the history and politics of the modern Middle East, are also emphasised.

Of special importance are the collections on the countries of the Arab Gulf (including Saudi Arabia and, to a lesser extent, Yemen and Iraq). Exeter University Library, in conjunction with the Documentation Unit of the Centre for Arab Gulf Studies, University of Exeter (*qv*), has accepted responsibility under the MELCOM Area Specialisation Scheme for the Arab Gulf, and the Library has amassed a collection of around 3000 volumes on the area, including 400+ works on the Gulf War of 1990–1991, and over 500 American PhD theses on the region.

No attempt is made to collect manuscripts, or material in Persian, Turkish or Hebrew (Biblical or Modern). The Library currently (1995) subscribes to about 75 periodicals on Middle Eastern Studies, and houses the extensive collection of Arab Gulf newspapers collected by the Centre for Arab Gulf Studies (see above).

Access (including Catalogue access): Access is available to all for reference but borrowing is limited mainly to academic and related staff, and students of Exeter University.

The University Library belongs to the Libertas Consortium and its entire monograph and periodical collections (including all material in Arabic) have been catalogued in MARC format; the full Catalogue can be consulted via the Internet. The University Library has also developed a homepage on the World Wide Web which gives information on the Library's collections, and, via its subject trees, gives access to a wide range of bibliographical databases and hypertext links.

See: Auch. pp. 43–45, Pearson p. 118, Roper 3 pp. 464–465.

MASS: Arabian Peninsula [Exeter does not collect extensively vernacular periodicals or works of literature]; Iraq [Monographs only].

GLASGOW

Glasgow University Library   ■

Address:	Glasgow University Library,
	Hillhead Street,
	Glasgow G12 8QE
Tel:	0141 3398855
Fax:	0141 3304952
e-mail:	gxlx63@lib.gla.ac.uk

The University was allocated an annual grant for a chair in Oriental languages in 1708 by Queen Anne, and since that time Arabic was added to the other principal Semitic languages which had already been taught since the 16th Century. This chair was later, in the 19th Century, to be occupied by a number of distinguished scholars, among them James Robertson and W.B. Stevenson. Arabic was later taught in a separate Department of Arabic and Islamic Studies, which attracted a steady stream of postgraduate students; the Arabic language and literature sections of the Library were maintained principally to support teaching and research in that Department.

The Library's collections have been enriched at various times by several generous gifts and bequests. Under the terms of the will of Dr. William Hunter the University received, in 1807, all of his invaluable collections, which now form the Hunterian Museum. Hunter's library, in addition to many outstanding mediaeval manuscripts, also contained some 130 manuscripts in Arabic, Persian and Turkish. Dr. A.B. McGrigor gave his collection of books on Palestine in the 1930s, to be followed closely by the donation by Professors Robertson and Stevenson of their respective oriental libraries.

In 1979 some 200 Arabic books, mainly relating to early Arabic poetry, were purchased from Mr Abdul Karim, a postgraduate student who was returning to Iraq.

Approximate numbers of books and manuscripts:

Manuscripts-Hunterian: Arabic 64; Persian 32; Turkish 34.

Manuscripts-Non-Hunterian: Arabic 19; Persian 19; Ottoman firmans 7; Malay (Jawi) 2; Urdu 3.

Farmer Collection: Approximately 1600 volumes (manuscript and printed) of Oriental works, music and general literature, presented by Dr. Henry George Farmer (mainly on Middle Eastern and martial music).

Printed Books-Early: In addition to several early grammatical works on the Arabic language preserved in the 'Old Library', i.e. the Library as it was in 1790, Glasgow University possesses some 50 early topographical works relating to Palestine from the personal library of the German Biblical scholar, Konstantin von Tischendorf.

Printed Books-Modern: The breakdown of the modern collections of classified and pressmarked books is approximately as follows: Islam (religion) 350 vols.; Arabic language and literature 1080 vols.; Middle East history (including politics and economics) 1150 vols.; Middle Eastern archaeology 600 vols.

Access: All manuscripts and early printed books are housed in closed access stacks in the Special Collections Department. All modern books are available on open access. Access is available to the University Library to all members of the University free of charge, to graduates of all Scottish universities on payment of an appropriate fee, and to others at the discretion of the Librarian. Consultation rights are available under the terms of the Library Licence in appropriate circumstances. All applications for membership should be addressed in writing to the Librarian.

See: Auch. pp. 78–80; MWP p. 373, Pearson pp. 61, 93, 145, 173, 320, Roman pp. 47–49, Roper 3 pp. 465–466.

See also: J. Young & P. Henderson Aitken, *A Catalogue of the Manuscripts in the Library of the Hunterian Museum in the University of Glasgow*; James Robson, 'Catalogue of the Oriental Mss in the Library of the University of Glasgow' in C.J. Mullo Weir (ed.), *Presentation Volume to William Barron Stevenson*, pp. 116–137.

Mitchell Library ■

Address:	Mitchell Library,
	North Street,
	Glasgow G3 7DN
Tel:	0141 287 2999
Fax:	0141 287 2815

The Mitchell Library maintains no separate Islamic or Middle Eastern Collections. However, as a large public reference library, it can supply a range of material on the subject from the Arts Department, the History and Glasgow Room and the Social Sciences Department.

Approximate numbers of books: Islam c.700; Arabic language 77; Arabic language audio course 10; Arabic literature 25; Middle East history 931; Middle East travel 626; Arab Gulf (geography) 272; Arab Gulf (history) 369.

Access: The Mitchell Library is open to all members of the public.

HULL

■ Brynmor Jones Library, University of Hull

Address:	Brynmor Jones Library,
	The University of Hull,
	Hull HU6 7RX
Tel:	01482 346311
Fax:	01482 466205
Telex:	9312134728 HU G
e-mail:	m.nicholson@lib.hull.ac.uk

The Library does not have any special collections on Islam and the Middle East, but the South-East Asia collection includes material on Islam. The University Archives include the Perronet Thompson and Sykes Papers, and the Hotham and Chichester Papers formerly in Humberside County Record Office.

Approximate numbers of books: Periodicals c.25 titles; Islam 500; Middle East history 1900; Politics 150; Social Sciences 250; Geography 40; Anthropology 80; Arabic language and literature 110.

Access: The Library is open to members of the University of Hull, to members of other British universities during vacations and to other researchers at the discretion of the Librarian. The archives section is open to visitors by appointment.

See: Jones p. 219, MWP pp. 224–225, 271–272, Roman p. 43, Roper 3 pp. 466–467.
See also: The Library's publication *Recent Accessions in the Field of South-East Asian Studies*, published twice yearly in February and August, which includes items on Islam in South East Asia.

■ Hull University Library

See under: HULL: Brynmor Jones Library, University of Hull

LANCASTER

Lancaster University Library   ■

Address: Lancaster University Library,
             Lancaster LA1 4YH
Tel: 01524 592536
Fax: 01524 65719

The University Library began to acquire Arabic, Islamic and Middle Eastern material in 1972 to support courses offered by the Department of Arabic and Islamic Studies. The Department ceased teaching in the early 1980s and current interests in this area are now the responsibility of the Department of Religious Studies and the Department of Politics and International Relations.

Access: Access is available to all members of Lancaster University. Members of other academic institutions wishing to use the Library should first contact the Sub-Librarian (Reader Services).

LEEDS

■   ## Brotherton Library, University of Leeds

Address:	The Brotherton Library,
	University of Leeds,
	Leeds LS2 9JT
Tel:	0113 233 5517
Fax:	0113 233 5561
e-mail:	m.c.davis@leeds.ac.uk
JANET:	leeds.library *Or* 000012006000

The Islamic and Middle Eastern collections have been built up chiefly during the past 50 years by means of recommended purchases and donations. Since October 1991 all newly-acquired books have been entered in the Computer Catalogue, and work is in progress on the retrospective conversion of earlier records to machine-readable form.

Until the early 1980s the Department of Semitic Studies concentrated chiefly on Hebrew and related studies, but since that time there has been a shift in emphasis towards Arabic studies, and in 1985 the Department was renamed The Department of Modern Arabic Studies. In 1996 it changed its name again to The Department of Arabic and Middle Eastern Studies. The University Library has attracted several substantial collections of Arabic donations since that time and current purchasing concentrates on Arabic and related subjects, but major works relevant to Hebrew Studies are still acquired to update the holdings in the older spheres of study and research. Material relevant to Middle Eastern history, politics, philosophy and theology is also acquired, mainly in Western languages. In 1992 the Department's substantial library was disbanded, non-duplicate books were transferred to the Brotherton, and the collection of several hundreds of Arabic, Hebrew, Persian, Urdu, Samaritan and Malay Mss acquired by a former Head of the Department, Dr. John Bowman, for teaching purposes was transferred to Special Collections.

Approximate numbers of books: Islam worldwide c.1000; Arabic language and literature c.4500; Middle East history c.1000 (microfilms of source materials relevant to late 19th and early 20th century British policy in the Middle East have greatly strengthened holdings in this area); Hebrew and Judaica – at least 20,000 items of which the principal components are: (a) c.6000 vols. of periodicals and printed books, and (b) the Roth Collection which comprises about 10,000 separate items (including c.350 Mss, c.1000 rare books, c.6000 vols. of periodicals and printed books, several thousand pamphlets of which many are offprints, and letters from and to Cecil Roth). A project to catalogue the hitherto uncatalogued pamphlets has just commenced.

Access: Serious research workers are allowed access to the Library on written application to the University Librarian.

See: Jones p. 221, MWP pp. 277–278, Pearson pp. 60, 93, 129, 317, Roman pp. 42–43 [the information contained here about the Dept. of Semitic Studies – now the Department of Arabic and Middle Eastern Studies – is out of date], Roper 3 pp. 467–469.
See also: Saul Lieberman (ed.), *Alexander Max: Jubilee Volume* for a listing by Dr. Roth of Roth's Mss; M.C. Davis, *A Catalogue of the Pre-1850 Books in the Cecil Roth Collection.*

Leeds University Library   ■

See under: LEEDS: Brotherton Library, University of Leeds.

The Liddle Collection, Brotherton Library, University of Leeds   ■

Address:	The Liddle Collection,
	Brotherton Library,
	University of Leeds,
	Leeds LS2 9JT
Tel:	0113 233 5566
Fax:	0113 233 5561
e-mail:	p.h.liddle@leeds.ac.uk

Within a comprehensive archive of British and some foreign personal experience documentation, covering 1914–1918 and beyond those central terms of reference, there is a remarkably rich Middle Eastern section. It consists of original papers, documents, letters, diaries, tape recordings and photos, all relating to personal experience in the 1914–18 War. A great deal of the material relates to the Middle East, in particular to Egypt, Palestine, Jordan, Syria,

Lebanon and Iraq, but also to the Gulf. There is also a book collection attached to the archive and a considerable amount of 1939–45 North African and Palestine material.

Access: Enquiries and correspondence regarding the Archive are welcomed by the Keeper and his assistant, and visitors to the archive will be guaranteed a warm welcome.

LEICESTER

The Islamic Foundation Library   ■

Address: The Islamic Foundation Library,
           Markfield Dawah Centre,
           Ratby Lane,
           Markfield, Leicester.
Tel: 01530 244944/5
Fax: 01530 244946

The Library was established in 1973 with the inception of the Islamic Foundation in that year. At present it consists of a Book section and a Journal Section. The Library concentrates mainly on Islamic subjects (i.e. Qur'an, Hadith, Islamic history, Fiqh, Politics, Philosophy, Islamic Resurgence, Profiles of individual Muslim Countries, Islamic Art and Architecture, Arabic literature). There is a small collection of books on general subjects (e.g. Sociology, Politics, History etc.) as well as all important polyglot dictionaries, well-known encyclopaedias, and a few year-books.

Apart from the Main Library, there are collections on relevant fields in the following units of the Foundation:

1 Inter-Faith Unit (Christian–Muslim Relations)
2 Islamic Economics Unit
3 Muslims of Central Asia Unit

A small Documentation Unit is housed in the Main Library and it consists of conference papers, reports etc. as well as some newspaper clippings on a limited number of topics relevant to the Muslim World in general and Muslims in Britain in particular. Approximate numbers of books and journals in the Main Library:

Books: Arabic 3000; Urdu 2000; English 12,000; Other Languages 1000.
Journals: Arabic 30 titles (some of these with back issues from 1973–); Urdu 15 titles (some of these with back issues from 1973–); English 150 titles (most of these with back issues from 1973–)

Access: The Library is open to all for reference only. Photocopying facilities are available. Microfiche and microfilm readers are also available.

LIVERPOOL

■ Liverpool University Library

See under: LIVERPOOL: Sydney Jones Library, University of Liverpool.

■ Sydney Jones Library, University of Liverpool

Address:	Sydney Jones Library,
	The University of Liverpool,
	PO Box 123,
	Liverpool L69 3DA
Tel:	0151 7942684
Fax:	0151 7942681
Telex:	627095 UNILPL G
e-mail:	library@liverpool.ac.uk

The sections of the University Library which most concern this Directory are the Sydney Jones Library (Arts and Social Sciences) and the Archaeology Library which is a departmental library administered from the Sydney Jones Library. The Middle East Collections reflect the undergraduate teaching programme which concentrates on the ancient languages (primarily Egyptian, Hebrew and Akkadian, also Coptic and Aramaic) and cultures of the Near and Middle East rather than the modern side. However, a course on contemporary Middle East history has recently been established.

Approximate numbers of books: (a) Sydney Jones Library: Middle East history c.2150 vols.; (b) Archaeology Library: Archaeology of the Middle East and Egypt c.3725 vols.; Ancient languages of the Middle East and Egypt c.3515 vols.; Art and Architecture of the Middle East and Egypt c.305 vols.; (c) Sydney Jones Library: Subjects as in (b) c.1800 vols. (the Archaeology Library is nearly full and little has been added in the last 12 years).

Access: Non-members of the University who would like to consult the collections should apply to Reader Services, Sydney Jones Library.

See: Jones p. 221, MWP p. 283, Pearson pp. 60, 93, 117, 318, Roper 3 p. 470.

LONDON

The Arab-British Centre Library   ■

Address:	The Arab-British Centre Library,
	21, Collingham Road,
	London SW5 0NU
Tel:	0171 373 8414
Fax:	0171 835 2088

The origins of the Library of the Arab-British Centre (ABC) go back to 1967, but the ABC itself was only opened in July 1977. While it contains material on the whole of the Arab world, about sixty per cent of the collection is concerned with the Palestine/Israel conflict. It is almost exclusively an English language library, with only a few volumes in Arabic. Almost all the books are of recent date. There is a small collection dealing with each of the countries of the Arab Gulf.

Approximate numbers of books: There are 1750 books in the Library. In addition, there are a small collection of pamphlets and a large number of periodicals and specialist magazines. The Library keeps press cuttings on the Middle East from the British quality press going back to 1967.

Access: Anyone may use the Library for reference; no borrowing is permitted.

Bible Society Library   ■

See under: CAMBRIDGE: Bible Society's Collections.

British and Foreign Bible Society Library   ■

See under: CAMBRIDGE: Bible Society's Collections.

■ BBC World Service Information Centre

Address:	BBC World Service Information Centre,
	Bush House,
	PO Box 76,
	Strand,
	London WC2B 4PH
Tel:	0171 257 2047
Fax:	0171 497 8156

The Information Centre provides a comprehensive, 24-hour information service to BBC World Service programme makers. Parts of both the books and press cuttings collections cover Islamic and Middle Eastern issues.

Access: Access is restricted to BBC programme makers only.

■ The British Library

Address:	Oriental and India Office Collections,
	The British Library,
	197, Blackfriars Road,
	London SE1 8NG.
	NB: The Library began moving its collections to its new building at St. Pancras, London, in December 1996. The move is scheduled to take two and a half years. Since this Directory appears during the actual period of the move, potential users of the Library's Oriental and India Office Collections are urged to check on the location of the books etc. which they require, by telephone, *in advance* of any visit. Recorded information about the move, which will be updated regularly, is available on 0171 412 7072.
Tel:	0171 412 7873 (general enquiries)
Fax:	0171 412 7858 (general fax)
	0171 412 7641 (enquiries by fax)
e-mail:	oioc-enquiries@bl.uk (for enquiries)
WWW:	http://portico.bl.uk/ [This will hold increasingly detailed information about the move to the St. Pancras site as it becomes available]

Nature and Scope of the Collections

There is no Islamic or Middle Eastern Collection as such: the British Library acquires and catalogues works on the humanities and social sciences by language rather than by subject (with the exception of South Asia). For material of Middle Eastern interest held elsewhere in the Library, the reader is referred to the relevant paragraph below.

The Oriental and India Office Collections of the British Library (OIOC) were brought together in 1991. OIOC has taken over, from the former Department of Oriental Manuscripts and Printed Books, responsibility for the Library's holdings in the languages of Asia and of North and North East Africa covering the humanities and social and political sciences. The India Office Library and Records Collections reflect the interests and activities of the East India Company and the India Office, and include documents and publications on South Asia, the Gulf area, Central Asia, South East Asia and the Far East.

Oriental – Language Holdings

The Oriental Collections' origins lie in the oriental-language manuscripts and printed books of the British Museum, founded in 1753. With the complementary collections of the India Office Library, the Department holds about 65,000 oriental manuscripts (and thousands more fragments in the Stein, Genizah and other collections), 900,000 printed books in oriental languages, and about 120,000 volumes of oriental periodicals and newspapers. There are impressive numbers of early imprints, but the main emphasis now is on acquiring new monographs and serials, official publications and other material for the study of all aspects of contemporary and traditional Asia and North Africa.

Approximate numbers of manuscripts and books of Middle Eastern interest: Arabic, Persian, Turkish, and the Iranian and Turkic languages of Central Asia: c.19,000 mss, c.110,000 printed books (with the India Office Library material); Hebrew including Samaritan: over 3000 mss, and 10,000 Cairo Genizah fragments; Printed books in Hebrew and Yiddish: c.75,000.

India Office Records

The India Office Records comprise the archives of the East India Company (1600–1858), the Board of Control (1784–1858), India

Office (1858–1947), Burma Office (1937–1948), and a number of British agencies overseas. They form a unique source for the history of British trade and government in South Asia and neighbouring areas. The India Office Records are available to the public under the Public Records Acts. For their history and arrangement, see M. Moir, *A General Guide to the India Office Records*. There are also about 70,000 maps, both manuscript and printed.

Prints and Drawings
From the India Office Library, OIOC has inherited an unrivalled collection of paintings and drawings from India by British and Indian artists, plus Persian and Indian miniatures (overall about 30,000 items). There are also more than 200,000 original photographs. Prints and Drawings material may be viewed by appointment in the Prints and Drawings Room.

Related Material Elsewhere in the British Library
Western-language material of interest to OIOC users may also be found in the general printed books collections, the Department of Manuscripts, the Music Library, the Map Library, and the Official Publications and Social Sciences Service, as well as the Philatelic Collections. Modern scientific and technological literature in some oriental languages is held by the Science Reference and Information Service (25, Southampton Buildings, Chancery Lane, London WC2A 1AX; Tel: 0171 323 7494).

Western-language newspapers from Asia may be consulted at the Newspaper Library (Colindale Avenue, London NW9 5HE; Tel: 0171 323 7353) and Asian recorded music at the National Sound Archive (29, Exhibition Road, London SW7 2AS; Tel: 0171 589 6603).

Access: Material cannot be borrowed from the British Library except for certain categories of publication which are available through inter-library loan. Access to the OIOC is granted to scholars and research students, and to those members of the public who have a serious interest in the collections and wish to work on them.

See: Auch. pp. 23–29, Jones p. 217, MWP pp. 4–71, Pearson pp. 51–53, 57, 89–90, 115–116, 142–143, 172, 185, 303–307, Roman pp. 7–23, Roper 3 pp. 471–490.

See also: A.G. Ellis, *Catalogue of Arabic Books in the British Museum* (vols. 1–2), A.S. Fulton, *Indexes* [to the above] (vol. 3); A.S. Fulton & A.G. Ellis, *Supplementary Catalogue of Arabic Printed Books in the British Museum*; A.S. Fulton & M. Lings, *Second Supplementary Catalogue of Arabic Printed Books in the British Museum 1926–1957*; M. Lings & Y.H. Safadi, *Third Supplementary Catalogue of Arabic Printed Books in the British Library 1958–1969* (4 vols.); G. Margoliouth, *Catalogue of the Hebrew and Samaritan Manuscripts in the British Museum* (4 vols.); J. Zedner, *Catalogue of the Hebrew Books in the Library of the British Museum*. Among the more modern catalogues are: R. Vassie (ed.), *Handlist of Arabic Manuscripts Acquired Since 1912: Vol. 1: Islamic Law, Vol. 2: Qur'anic Sciences and Hadith*; U. Sims-Williams, *Handlist of Islamic Manuscripts Acquired by the India Office Library, 1938–1985;* idem., *Catalogue of the Arabic Manuscripts in the Library of the India Office, Vol. 2: Index;* idem., *Union Catalogue of Persian Serials and Newspapers in British Libraries*; M.I. Waley (ed.), *Periodicals in Turkish and Turkic Languages: A Union List of Holdings in UK Libraries*; D. Rowland-Smith (ed.), *Second Supplementary Catalogue of Hebrew Printed Books in the British Library, 1893–1960* (2 vols.).

MASS: Arabian Peninsula, Jordan, Lebanon, Syria.

British Library of Political and Economic Science   ■

Address:	British Library of Political and Economic Science,
	London School of Economics and Political Science,
	University of London,
	10, Portugal Street,
	London WC2A 2HD
Tel:	0171 405 7686
Telex:	24655 BLPES G

The Library was founded in 1896 to serve not only as the working library of the London School of Economics but also as a national collection. It has maintained a research collection in the fields of economics, politics and sociology published in modern European languages and in Russian.

It is impossible to quantify the proportion of material relating to the Middle East; but the total stock contains nearly four million items, with some 750,000 bound volumes, including over 450,000 pamphlets, and over 24,000 serials of which over 9000 are received currently. The Library has a particularly strong collection of the documents of local, regional, national and international governmental organisations. A *London Bibliography of the Social Sciences* (the printed version of the subject catalogue) is published annually and is available as 'IBSS On-Line' via BIDS and on CD-ROM.

Access: For admission, apply to the Circulation Supervisor. A fee may be charged.

See: Jones p. 217, MWP p. 71, Roper 3 p. 495.

■   ## British Museum Ethnography Library

Address:	British Museum Ethnography Library,
	Department of Ethnography,
	British Museum,
	Museum of Mankind,
	Burlington Gardens,
	London W1X 2EX
Tel:	0171 323 8031
Fax:	0171 323 8013

The Library includes the former Library of the Royal Anthropological Institute (RAI) which was given on trust to the British Museum in 1976, and incorporated into the Ethnography departmental library. The Institute continues to donate books to the Library to keep the loan stock up to date. The stock is composed of books, pamphlets and serials dealing with social anthropology, ethnography and, more selectively, associated sciences such as archaeology, biological anthropology, linguistics, medical anthropology etc. There is also a large collection of mainly 19th Century travel books.

Approximate numbers of Books: Middle East 3000–4000 books and journals; Islam and Islamic countries 10–15,000 books and journals. There is also a small collection of books dealing with the Arab Gulf.

Manuscripts: The Library itself has no manuscript collection, all British Museum manuscripts having been transferred to the British Library (*qv*), when the latter was founded. The Manuscript and Archive Collection of the RAI is housed in the Museum of Mankind building and a catalogue is available for consultation in the

Reading Room. Applications to consult manuscripts in this Collection should be addressed to the RAI Representative at the above address.

The Burton Collection: The Burton Collection or Library, located for some time at the British Museum Ethnography Library, was never owned by the latter. It was eventually sold by the RAI to the Huntington Library in the USA.

Access: The Library is a library of last resort. Reference tickets or day passes are granted to bona fide researchers to consult material not available elsewhere. RAI Fellows are eligible for a special loan ticket which allows them to borrow books and journals donated by the RAI. Applicants are required to produce a passport sized photograph and the name of a referee. Applicants for a day pass are required to produce proof of identity and home address. For the consultation of manuscripts, see above.

See: Jones p. 224.

British Standards Institution Library   ■

Address:	The Library,
	British Standards Institution,
	389, Chiswick High Road,
	London W4 4AL
Tel:	0181 996 9000 (BSI)
	0181 996 7004 (Library)
Fax:	0181 996 7048

The coverage of the Library of the British Standards Institution (BSI) embraces national standards and related technical documents from Europe, USA, Canada, Australasia, Japan, China, India, Saudi Arabia, South Africa, Malaysia and Singapore. Standards catalogues are held for many other countries, including most Middle Eastern and African countries. Some English translations are held. International and European standards, including GCC (Gulf Cooperation Council), are also held.

Access (including databases): The Library is open to BSI members. Non-members will be charged a fee.

There is access to various on-line systems including Dialog, Datastar, and Eurobases. CD-Roms held include PERINORM, JUSTIS CELEX, EUROLAW,

WWSS, DODISS PLUS and Federal Register. It is hoped to have Internet access in the near future.

Loans Service: A Loans Service is in operation which 'provides a quick method of gaining sight of foreign standards and other documents for a nominal charge'. This service is available to BSI subscribing members and permits the loan of 'Foreign and International standards, regulations and technical specifications, including official translations where held. Exceptions are British Standards, international equivalents of BSs, and some publications held for reference only.' Potential users may request to borrow documents by means of telephone, fax or letter, or during a personal visit. Telephone requests are limited to five documents at a time since their availability has to be checked.

■   Chatham House Library

See under: LONDON: Royal Institute of International Affairs Library.

■   Euston Centre Library, University of Westminster

Address:	Euston Centre Library,
	University of Westminster,
	9–18, Euston Centre,
	London NW1 3ET
Tel:	0171 911 5000 ext. 4347
Telex:	25964

The Library supports the teaching and learning needs of Arabic at all the levels taught in the University. There are c.4000 books and 21 current periodical subscriptions. The dictionaries collection numbers c.200, and includes specialist and technical dictionaries.

Access: Access to the Library for reference purposes is permitted to members of other higher education institutions, and may be extended to other categories of user by arrangement.

Foreign and Commonwealth Office Library   ■

Address:	Foreign and Commonwealth Office Library,
	Room E213,
	King Charles Street,
	London SW1A 2AH
Tel:	0171 270 3925/3919
Fax:	0171 270 3682
	0171 930 2364
e-mail:	fcoafric@clusl.ulcc.ac.uk

Material on the Middle East in the FCO Library forms part of the Library's general collection on world affairs and international relations, dating mainly from the 19th and 20th Centuries. The historical collection is strongest in those areas which in the past have been particularly associated with the UK, e.g. Aden, Iraq, the Gulf States, Jordan, Israel etc. The main subjects covered are administration, description and travel, economics, foreign relations, history, law and politics of all countries, regional organisations, Islam (worldwide).

Access: Access for reference purposes is by appointment only.

See: MWP pp. 79–80.
See also: Foreign Office, *Catalogue of Printed Books in the Library of the Foreign Office*; idem., *Catalogue of the Foreign Office Library, 1926–1968*.

Al-Furqan Islamic Heritage Foundation Library   ■

Address:	The Library,
	Al-Furqan Islamic Heritage Foundation,
	Eagle House,
	High Street,
	Wimbledon,
	London SW19 5EF
Tel:	0181 944 1233
Fax:	0181 944 1633
Telex:	925447 FURQAN G

The Foundation is situated in an imposing 17th Century Jacobean House. The principal concern of the Foundation is 'the preservation of the cultural heritage embodied in Islamic manuscripts'. It exists 'to promote the study, cataloguing, publication, preservation and conservation of Islamic manuscripts throughout the world'. Thus, Al-Furqan Islamic Heritage Foundation includes in its activities (in the words of its *Newsletter*, No. 1 (September 1995), p. 3):

- conducting a worldwide survey of all libraries with Islamic manuscripts;
- the study and cataloguing of collections of Islamic manuscripts that have never been catalogued;
- the documentation (imaging) of Islamic manuscripts, using the best available technological means;
- editing and publishing a wide selection of important manuscripts.

To support its research, especially that relating to manuscripts, the Foundation has established a Reference Library. In 1995 this contained over 10,000 volumes, expected to rise to 15,000, covering the major aspects of Islamic Studies in all the principal Islamic languages. Areas covered include architecture, law, literature, science, history, medicine and geography. The *Newsletter* (p. 16) describes the Library as follows:

> The Library has recorded its collection on a bi-alphabetic automated catalogue which displays bibliographical data in the Arabic script as well as the Roman script, including the transliteration of all major Islamic languages. This database, developed exclusively for the Foundation, possesses many versatile and outstanding features: all fields of a bibliographical record can be searched in both scripts, and various reports generated from the database can be printed. The entire collection is available on open shelves (classified by the Library of Congress scheme) for ease of use.
>
> The Library staff are committed to an on-going programme of acquisitions of all important reference material, both in Islamic and European languages. As a result, researchers will find the collection an invaluable source of documentation for their work.
>
> The Library also subscribes to a wide range of specialist journals in various languages. A detailed acquisitions list of the Library collection is also available. A complete catalogue of books and periodicals will be prepared at a later stage.

Access: Scholars and students who wish to use the Library should make written application to the Foundation.

See: Roper 3 pp. 491–492.

Guildhall Library   ■

Address:	Guildhall Library,
	Aldermanbury,
	London EC2P 2EJ
Tel:	0171 332 1868/1870 (Printed Books)
	0171 332 1863 (Manuscripts)

The Library specialises in the history of London but its collections cover a wide variety of subjects. In the Printed Books Section are approximately 100 items on subjects including Islamic Studies, Hebrew, travel and the historic role of Britain in the Middle East.

The Manuscripts Section includes the records of a number of companies which traded in the Middle East: Baghdad Light and Power Co.; Gray, Mackenzie and Co.; Levant Co.; John March; Ottoman Bank.

The Section also holds baptismal, marriage and death records for a number of British communities in the Middle East: those in Aden, Egypt, Iran, Iraq, Israel (Palestine), Kuwait, Lebanon, Libya, Syria, Turkey.

Access: Both Sections of the Library are open to all without requirement of ticket or letters of recommendation. The collections are for reference use only.

Horniman Museum and Library   ■

Address:	The Horniman Museum and Library,
	100 London Road,
	Forest Hill,
	London SE23 3PQ
Tel:	0181 699 1872 ext. 108
Fax:	0181 291 5506
e-mail:	horniman@demon.co.uk

The Middle Eastern and Islamic collections form part of the collection of topographical and travel works amassed by F.J. Horniman and his son E.J. Horniman mainly between 1880 and 1920. The collections have been added to since then in the fields of anthropology, ethnography, musicology and natural history. Most of the Middle Eastern works are published in English, none in Arabic. Many of the books describe material culture and customs in Islamic countries and also those countries with sizeable Islamic populations. A restricted number of books deal with the Gulf States.

Approximate numbers of books: About 1000 of the total 20,000 monographs deal with Islamic topics.

Access: The Library is open to the public for reference use without appointment.

See: Pearson pp. 117, 314.

■ House of Lords Record Office

Address:	The Record Office,
	House of Lords,
	London SW1A 0PW
Tel:	0171 219 3074
Fax:	0171 219 2570

The House of Lords Record Office has the custody of the records of both Houses of Parliament. They date from 1497 to the present day and have been preserved at Westminster since the 16th Century. The Commons Records were destroyed by fire in 1834 except for the original manuscript Journals (1547–1800) and a few stray documents. The Lords records include Acts of Parliament from 1497, the Lords Journals dating from 1510, and an increasing number of classes of record from the 17th Century. In addition, there are 'historical collections' or private papers which have accumulated through gift or purchase.

Records of the period from 1497 to 1693 have been calendared in the *Reports* of the Historical Manuscripts Commission and from 1693 to 1718 in a new series published for the House of Lords. For the subsequent period, the printed *Lords Journals*, which have separate collected indexes, indicate the date of each item of business in the House and manuscript lists indicate what documents survive. Abstracts from these calendars and lists relevant to certain areas throughout the world which include Arabic and Islamic countries have been collected and published in the guides noted below (*sv* **See also**).

Most of the Lords documents referred to in these guides relate to commerce and trade, particularly the slave trade, politics and war with the respective countries. Some historical material mainly relating to the First World War and the interwar period can be found in the political papers of Viscount Samuel, who was High Commissioner for Palestine, 1920–1925, David Lloyd George, Bonar Law and Viscount Stansgate. The Samuel Papers include letters from King Abdulla of Jordan as well as photocopies of the Palestinian papers which were deposited in the Israeli State Archives in 1963.

In addition to manuscript material, there are some relevant papers amongst the printed Lords and Commons *Sessional Papers* for the 19th and 20th Centuries, such as the papers relating to the arrangements made between the Porte and Mehmet Ali in 1833 (*HC Sessional Papers*, 1839 Vol.L). These can be consulted in the Record Office Search Room given forty-eight hours notice. All accessions since 1971 are listed in the published annual reports of the Office and handlists of the Samuel and Stansgate Papers have also been published. All are available for a fee from the Record Office.

Access: Visitors are requested to make an appointment. The Record Office is closed for annual stocktaking in the last two weeks of November.

See also: MWP; J.D. Pearson, *Guide to Manuscripts and Documents in the British Isles Relating to Africa* (2 vols.). A comprehensive *Guide to the Records of Parliament* by Maurice F. Bond can be obtained from the House of Lords Record Office for a fee.

Hulton Deutsch Collection   ■

Address:	Hulton Deutsch Collection,
	21–31, Woodfield Road,
	London W9 2BA
Tel:	0171 266 2660
Fax:	0171 266 2414
WWW:	http://www.u-net.com/hulton

The Library is a commercial picture library containing some 15 million images in all kinds of media up to the year 1957. Subjects include Islamic and Middle East history and the materials are arranged by specific subject. There are no books or documents, and comparatively little colour material.

Access: Enquiries are welcome from people with Islamic and Middle Eastern interests. As a commercial library, the Hulton Deutsch Collection is not open for pure research: users must have a particular publishing project, film or TV programme in mind. A scale of fees is available on request. It is possible to borrow pictures by post for reference.

■ Imperial War Museum

Address:	Imperial War Museum,
	Lambeth Road,
	London SE1 6HZ
Tel:	0171 416 5000 (Museum)
	0171 416 5221/5222/5223 (Department of Documents)
	0171 416 5342/5343/5344 (Department of Printed Books)
Fax:	0171 416 5374

The Department of Documents has among its collections the papers of many British men and women who have served in the Middle East since 1914. These include the records of several prominent commanders from both World Wars, most notably Field Marshal Lord Chetwode, Major General G.F. Dawnay, Lieutenant General Sir Oliver Leese, Major General D.L. Lloyd-Owen, Field Marshal Viscount Montgomery of Alamein and General Sir Archibald Murray. The Department's holdings also contain the personal diaries, letters and unpublished memoirs of many junior officers and men, of all three services, who fought at Gallipoli and in Palestine and Mesopotamia during the First World War, and in the Middle East and North Africa in the 1939–45 War.

The Department of Printed Books (which constitutes a national reference library with well over 100,000 books, 30,000 pamphlets, 15,000 volumes of periodicals and 20,000 maps and technical drawings) has a fairly extensive collection of books, pamphlets, journals and maps dealing with conflict in the Middle East in the 20th Century. Although the bulk of the material is in Western European languages, there are some Arabic and Turkish items. The Department has an active reprint publishing programme which includes British official histories of military operations in Egypt, Palestine, Turkey and Persia during the First World War.

Access: At least 24 hours notice should be given of intended visits to both the above Departments. Visitors with appointments are admitted free to these Departments, but there is a charge for touring the Museum's galleries before 4.30 pm. The Departments are closed for annual stocktaking for the whole of the last two full weeks in November.

See: Jones p. 219, MWP pp. 91–94.

India Office Library and Records   ■

See under: LONDON: The British Library.

Institute of Archaeology Library   ■

Address:	Institute of Archaeology Library,
	31–34, Gordon Square,
	London WC1H 0PY
Tel:	0171 387 7050 ext. 7485
Fax:	0171 380 7373/7727
e-mail:	library@ucl.ac.uk

The Library has no special Islamic collection but has a good section on Middle East archaeology and holds the excavation records of some Middle East sites.

Access: Prospective users who are not members of London University should address their enquiries to the Librarian in the first instance.

See: Jones p. 220.

Institute of Commonwealth Studies Library   ■

Address:	Institute of Commonwealth Studies Library,
	University of London,
	28, Russell Square,
	London WC1B 5DS
Tel:	0171 580 5876
Fax:	0171 255 2160
e-mail:	icommlib@sas.ac.uk

The Collection dates from the foundation of the Institute in 1949 and covers those areas of the Middle East and the Mediterranean which are or were part of the Empire/Commonwealth or were administered by Britain. Materials are collected only for the period of British administration. The collection comprises books, periodicals, bibliographies, government publications (including Colonial Office and Foreign Office confidential prints) and documents issued by political parties and pressure groups (mostly relating to Malta and Cyprus since the 1960s). Parties represented by more than one or two documents include (from Cyprus) AKEL, the Centre Union, Democratic Rally, Edek Socialist Party, the National Unity Party (Northern Cyprus); and (from Malta) the Democratic Nationalist Party (Malta), the Maltese Labour Party, the Nationalist Party and the Progressive Constitutional Party. There are also two small archival collections relating to Aden and Cyprus.

The Library also maintains a register of research in progress and completed on Commonwealth topics for higher degrees of British universities. It publishes *Theses in Progress in Commonwealth Studies* and a quarterly list of new titles added to stock; the Middle East and Mediterranean section of the latter is available on request.

Approximate numbers of books: Middle East and Mediterranean 3000 books.

Access (including Catalogue access): Access is available to postgraduate and other advanced research workers from all countries and to undergraduates who can show a need for materials which cannot be obtained elsewhere. The Library shares a catalogue with the other member-Institutes of the University of London's School of Advanced Study. The Internet address for the system is 193.62.18.239.

■ Institute of Education Library

Address:	The Library and Media Services,
	Institute of Education,
	University of London,
	20, Bedford Way,
	London WC1H 0AL
Tel:	0171 612 6080
Fax:	0171 612 6093
e-mail:	libenquiries@ioe.ac.uk
JANET:	library.ioe.ac.uk

The Library and Media Services Department has the largest collection of books and other materials on education in the UK. It subscribes to about 1000 periodicals from all over the world on education and related subjects, and there is also a large multi-media collection of materials at school level. The Library subscribes to several CD-ROM services such as Australian/British/Canadian education indexes ('International ERIC'), ERIC, the International Centre for Distance Learning database, and UNESCO databases, and specialises in on-line searching in the fields of education and psychology.

Coverage of education overseas is concentrated on the countries of the Commonwealth, Europe and some parts of Latin America, reflecting in part the countries of origin of the large number of overseas staff and students.

The Library has a very small collection of material on the Arab and Islamic world since this is not an area which the Institute concentrates on. However, as noted, there is quite a lot of material on education in Commonwealth countries, and there is an overlap between the two.

Access: The collections are housed in a new, purpose-built building attached to the main Institute building in central London. The Library exists primarily to support the teaching and research needs of staff and students of the Institute, but welcomes use by others in the community who are interested in education. Application should be made in person at the main Issue Counter; visitors will be required to produce evidence of identity and sign the Visitors' Book on their first visit. A general enquiry service is available to personal callers only; although advice and guidance on appropriate sources are available, it is not possible to undertake complex bibliographical searches for readers. Use of other services (e.g. on-line searching and photocopying) is available on the basis of charges at the point of use.

Borrowing rights are available to **Associate Members**, on the payment of a subscription. This entitles the Associate Member to borrow three 'ordinary loan' items, from the main lending collections only. Special arrangements are made for academic and academic-related staff and research students of certain colleges and schools of the University of London.

■ Institute of Ismaili Studies Library

Address:	The Library, Institute of Ismaili Studies, 42–44, Grosvenor Gardens, London SW1W 0EB
Tel:	0171 881 6000
Fax:	0171 881 6040

The Institute of Ismaili Studies was established in 1977 with the object of promoting scholarship and learning on Muslim cultures and societies, historical as well as contemporary, and a better understanding of their relationship with other societies and faiths. Within the Islamic tradition, the Institute's programmes seek to promote research on those areas which have received relatively lesser attention in scholarship to date. These include the intellectual and literary expressions of Shiism in general, and Ismailism in particular.

The Library was established in 1979, and its role, directed by the Institute's intellectual mission and scope of activities, is twofold: to develop and make available, to scholars and students within and outside the Institute, a central archive of Ismaili manuscripts and printed materials; and to support the programmes of the Institute by providing the necessary textual and visual materials.

The Library has a core collection of reference works, periodicals, texts and studies on aspects of Islamic history, theology, philosophy, law and literature comprising nearly 20,000 items. The Library's unique collection of Ismaili materials, amongst the largest in the Western world, consists of manuscripts, printed books, articles and theses.

The Ismaili manuscript holdings comprise nearly 800 volumes, and provide indispensable source materials for scholars and students interested in Ismaili Studies. The non-Ismaili manuscript holdings total 450 volumes, and cover a variety of subjects including commentaries on the Qur'an, jurisprudence, theology, philosophy, history, biography, logic, medicine and alchemy.

Access: Access is available to postgraduate students, scholars and researchers, and to undergraduates who can show a need for materials not available elsewhere.

See: Roper 3 pp. 492–493.

See also: Adam Gacek, *Catalogue of Arabic Manuscripts in the Library of the Institute of Ismaili Studies* (2 vols.).

Institute of Jewish Affairs Library ■

Address:	Institute of Jewish Affairs Library,
	79, Wimpole Street,
	London W1M 7DD
Tel:	0171 935 8266
Fax:	0171 935 3252
e-mail:	ija@ort.ort

The Library contains 20,000 books and pamphlets, an archive of press cuttings and some 400 periodicals. Subjects covered include Human Rights, Antisemitism, Racism, the Holocaust and the Second World War, Christian-Jewish Relations, Eastern Europe and the former Soviet Union, the Middle East, Israel and the Arab–Israel Conflict.

Access: The Library is not open to the public but postgraduate researchers may visit by appointment only. Books may be borrowed on inter-library loan.

King's College Library ■

Address:	The Library,
	King's College London,
	Strand,
	London WC2R 2LS
Tel:	0171 873 2139/2140/2141
Fax:	0171 872 0207
e-mail:	library@bay.cc.kcl.ac.uk

The College has an Islamic collection to serve the BA degree in Religious Studies and some books on the Middle East to provide background for courses in Modern Greek and Byzantine History.

Access: Access is open for reference only to all members of London University. Others should apply by letter to the Director of Library Services.

■ Lambeth Palace Library

Address: Lambeth Palace Library,
            London SE1 7JU
Tel: 0171 928 6222

Archbishop Bancroft founded Lambeth Palace Library as a public library in 1610. It contains about 150,000 volumes of printed books as well as over 3000 volumes of manuscripts. Much of the collection deals with ecclesiastical history. The Library's collections with relevant Islamic and Middle Eastern materials include the Modern Archbishops' Papers (Tait-Ramsey), the Archbishop's Assyrian Mission, the Jerusalem and the East Mission and the Papers of G.F.P. Blyth, Bishop in Jerusalem.

Access: The Library is freely available to members of the public at the discretion of the Librarian. The Library has its entrance in Lambeth Palace Road about one hundred yards from the main gate of Lambeth Palace. New readers are asked to bring a letter of introduction from a person or institution of recognised standing. Special permission is needed for access to some categories of material, e.g. illuminated manuscripts.

See: Jones p. 220, MWP pp. 130–132, Pearson pp. 54, 93, 172, 314, Roper 3 pp. 494–495.

■ Leo Baeck College Library

Address: Leo Baeck College Library,
            80, East End Road,
            London N3 2SY
Tel: 0181 349 4525 ext. 400
Fax: 0181 343 4550

The Library has approximately 30,000 volumes in the field of Jewish Studies. There are substantial collections of the following subjects: Bible, Targum, Qumran, Rabbinic literature, Codes and Mediaeval commentaries, History, The Holocaust, Israel and Zionism. The whole of the sections on Rabbinic literature, and Codes and Mediaeval commentaries is available on CD-ROM. There is also a big collection of pamphlets on all the subjects mentioned above. In addition, the Library has a collection of microfilms of manuscripts and early printings which belonged to the Hochschule in Berlin (the training centre for progressive Judaism in Germany until it was closed by the Nazis).

Access: Anyone with a serious interest may use the Library by appointment.

Lincoln's Inn Library   ■

Address:	Lincoln's Inn Library,
	London WC2A 3TN
Tel:	0171 242 4371
Fax:	0171 831 1839

The Library, which is primarily a law library for barristers, has limited holdings in the areas covered by this Directory and no longer *collects* material from the Middle East or Islamic regions. However, its holdings include the following: about 100 textbooks on Islamic Law 1790–1980s, mainly as applied in India and Pakistan; some legislation from Persia, Palestine and the Gulf States when under British protection; *Law Reports of Palestine* 1920–1947; *Law Reports of Aden* 1937–1958; a few miscellaneous items on the law of Pakistan and Bangladesh.

Access: Admission to non-barristers is by appointment only.

London School of Economics Library   ■

See under: LONDON: British Library of Political and Economic Science.

London School of Hygiene and Tropical Medicine Library   ■

Address:	London School of Hygiene and Tropical Medicine Library,
	Keppel Street,
	London WC1E 7HT
Tel:	0171 927 2283
Fax:	0171 927 2273
Telex:	8953474
e-mail:	library@lshtm.ac.uk

The Library holds a selection of current medical and scientific periodicals published in the Middle East. The primary language is

English with one title in French and two in Turkish. The Library also receives three periodical titles from the World Health Organisation Regional Office for the Eastern Meditteranean. There are also runs of Middle Eastern periodicals which are no longer current. Many of these have been deposited with the Wellcome Institute for the History of Medicine Library (*qv*). The Library acquires books dealing with the public health and medicine of the area covered by this Directory. However, generally speaking, the type of medicine covered is Western rather than Islamic. The following are available on CD-ROM: Medline, Popline, Health-Plan.

Access (including Catalogue access): The Library is open for reference purposes to visitors wishing to consult its specialised collections. External membership for non-members of the School (allowing limited borrowing rights) is available on payment of both a refundable deposit and an annual fee. For further information please telephone the Librarian's Secretary.

The Library's catalogue of materials from 1980 onwards is available through the shared Libertas system of University College London. This may be consulted on the Internet via *http://www/ucl.ac.uk* or telnet *lib.ucl.ac.uk*.

■ The Middle East Association Reference Library and Information Centre

Address:	Middle East Association Reference Library and Information Centre, Bury House, 33, Bury Street, St. James's, London SW1Y 6AX
Tel:	0171 839 2137
Fax:	0171 839 6121

The Middle East Association is an independent private organisation established in 1961, now with about 300 UK members in a wide sector of economic activity. It is non-political and non-profit making, financed entirely by members' subscriptions. The Association's purpose is to promote trade between the UK and the Middle East (all Arab States plus Iran, Turkey, Afghanistan, Ethiopia and Eritrea). It offers members practical help towards increasing their business with these markets and monitoring developments. It also deals direct with enquiries and visitors from the Middle East.

The Reference Library and Information Centre provides a general enquiry service. The Library currently receives about 85 journals, including some newspapers and the newsletters of British Business Groups in the region. There are about 500 books, which include current trade directories, telephone directories, Yellow Pages, Kompass, economic reports and law reports as well as background material. There is a separate collection of monographs, UK and Middle East Government publications and those issued by British diplomatic missions overseas, pamphlets, newspaper cuttings, company reports and current laws of the countries covered.

Access: Members of the Association may have access to the Information Centre at any time; non-members by appointment. All the material is for reference only but photocopies may be made if appropriate. The staff of the Association, who have long experience of the area, are available to answer enquiries and to offer advice. They keep up to date by frequent visits and the close monitoring of all sources of information.

Middle East Economic Digest ■

Address:	Middle East Economic Digest,
	MEED House,
	21, John Street,
	London WC1N 2BP
Tel:	0171 404 5513
Fax:	0171 242 1450 (General)
	0171 831 9537 (Editorial)
	0171 430 0337 (Marketing)
Telex:	27165 MEEDAR G (Editorial)
	261456 MEEDAR G (General)

Middle East Economic Digest (MEED) no longer has a library. Publications are kept for a time but they are thrown out after a period due to lack of space. Books that are retained are kept to a minimum. MEED was taken over in 1987 by EMAP (East Midlands Allied Press) and *Africa Economic Digest* was sold.

Museum of Mankind Library ■

See under: LONDON: British Museum Ethnography Library.

■ National Art Library, Victoria and Albert Museum

Address:	National Art Library,
	Victoria and Albert Museum,
	Cromwell Road,
	South Kensington,
	London SW7 2RL
Tel:	0171 938 8315
Fax:	0171 938 8461
e-mail:	100316.3515@compuserve.com

The Library's Islamic collections have been gradually built up since the foundation of the Library in the mid-19th Century. As the National Art Library, the whole Library's role is to be as comprehensive as possible in all the fine and decorative arts. This applies to the Islamic material which is probably one of the finest collections of Islamic art books in the UK. The historical, geographical and topographical works on the Middle East are primarily to supplement the books on art subjects. Major reference works for Islamic Studies are held including dictionaries of most Middle Eastern languages, *The Encyclopaedia of Islam*, and various translations of the Qur'an. There are, however, very few books dealing with Arabic as a language, nor are there any documents dealing with the Gulf.

The Library is also a Museum Department holding objects. Among these are a large number of Islamic bookbindings (about 110), many of them of superlative quality, and bookbinding tools. There is also a collection of Arab, Persian and Turkish manuscripts, many of them illuminated, as well as some album leaves and examples of calligraphy. This is all fully catalogued in a bound xeroxed list available at the counter, and much of it is of great importance for any studies of the Islamic book. It is worth noting that a large number of Indian and Persian miniatures are kept in the Indian and South East Asian Collection. The National Art Library is also well supplied with past and current periodicals dealing with the Islamic arts.

Access: Access to the Library is available to the public.

See: MWP p. 214, Pearson pp. 54, 117, 145, 172, 314, Roper 3 p. 506.
See also: Duncan Haldane, *Islamic Bookbindings in the Victoria and Albert Museum*.

National Maritime Museum Library ■

Address: Library,
Maritime Information Centre (MIC),
National Maritime Museum,
London SE10 9NF
Tel: 0181 858 4422
Fax: 0181 312 6632

The Library possesses literature on Islamic subjects in the areas of navigation, astronomy and local craft. The following are available on CD-ROM: British Library Catalogue of Printed Books to 1975; British Humanities Index 1986 – to date; Current Technology Index 1986 – to date; Eighteenth Century Short Title Catalogue; Jane's Fighting Ships 1991–1992, 1993–1994; Jane's Naval Weapon Systems 1990.

Access: The Library is open to all over the age of 18, but those below this age may apply to use the Reading Room in special circumstances. All readers should obtain valid readers' tickets for admission to the Library.

See: Jones p. 223, MWP pp. 138–146.

National Register of Archives ■

Address: National Register of Archives,
Royal Commission on Historical Manuscripts,
Quality House,
Quality Court,
Chancery Lane,
London WC2A 1HP
Tel: 0171 242 1198
Fax: 0171 831 3550
e-mail: sargent@rsl-hr.sas.ac.uk

The National Register of Archives (NRA) was set up by the Commission in 1945 to collect and disseminate information about manuscript sources for British history outside the public records. This information is derived from unpublished lists and catalogues of manuscript collections received from repositories, and from various published sources. The Commission is not itself a record repository.

Information concerning Middle East history is normally collected only insofar as it relates to territories formerly under British rule, and it can be accessed through a number of computerised indexes. For instance, the Personal Index notes the location of surviving papers of administrators and diplomats who worked in these territories, the Subject Index notes some organisations which were associated with the Middle East, whilst the records of companies which had interests in that area may appear on the Business Index.

Access: These indexes can be consulted in the Commission's public search room, and it was intended that they should become available on the Internet during the course of 1995. In addition, limited and specific enquiries can be answered by post, fax or e-mail, although not by telephone.

See: Jones p. 223.

■ The National Sound Archive

See under: LONDON: The British Library.

■ The Newspaper Library

See under: LONDON: The British Library.

■ Palestine Exploration Fund Library

Address: The Library,
Palestine Exploration Fund,
2, Hinde Mews,
Marylebone Lane,
London W1M 5RR
Tel: 0171 935 5379

The Palestine Exploration Fund was founded in 1865 and has acquired its book collection over a number of years. The Library consists entirely of books on Palestine and its neighbours (including Cyprus, Lebanon, Syria and Arabia, with limited coverage of Anatolia, Egypt and Mesopotamia). The collection covers geography, environmental sciences, archaeology, architecture and history (secular and religious), and includes a fine collection of early travel books. Basic works on relevant ancient texts are held. The Fund also has extensive archival holdings, documentary, map and photographic, resulting from its 19th Century exploration and mapping of Palestine and its archaeological excavations from 1890–1935.

Approximate numbers of books: c.5000 books; Issues of 116 periodicals are held, 83 of which are currently taken.

Access: Subscribers to the Fund have borrowing rights. Members of the British School of Archaeology in Jerusalem and the British Institute at Amman for Archaeology and History may use the Library. Other serious enquirers are welcome to make a preliminary visit: it is advisable to telephone before visiting.

See: Jones pp. 160–161, MWP pp. 146–152.

Partnership House Mission Studies Library   ■

Address:	Partnership House Mission Studies Library,
	157, Waterloo Road,
	London SE1 8XA
Tel:	0171 928 8681

The Library was formed in 1988 by bringing together the post-1945 collections of the United Society for the Propagation of the Gospel (USPG) and the Church Mission Society (CMS). CMS's pre-1945 collection is also in the Library: it is called the Max Warren Collection in honour of the former General Secretary. USPG's pre-1945 collection is housed at Rhodes House Library, Oxford (*qv*).

The Library (post-1945 collection) has books and pamphlets on the Middle East, particularly on the Christian Churches and Islam, and also on Islam in those countries where the missionary societies are working, e.g. West and East Africa, India, East Asia and Europe (including the UK). They number about 400 items. The Max Warren Collection (pre-1945 collection) has books and pamphlets on the Middle East, particularly on the Christian Churches and Islam, and also on Islam in those countries where CMS has worked, e.g. West and East Africa, Iran and India. These number about 500 items, which are normally only available for reference.

Access: All interested in the history and theology of Christian mission are welcome to use the Library, free of charge. However, an annual subscription is charged to all who wish to borrow books, unless they are current or retired staff or missionaries of USPG or CMS.

■   ## Polytechnic of Central London Library

See under: LONDON: Euston Centre Library, University of Westminster.

■   ## Prince of Wales's Institute of Architecture Library

Address:	Prince of Wales's Institute of Architecture Library,
	14–15, Gloucester Gate,
	London NW1 6HG
Tel:	0171 916 7380
Fax:	0171 916 7381

The Library was established at the opening of the Institute in October 1992, based on the collection of the late John Julius Stanton, Head of History at Worth Abbey. It has been expanded through gifts and purchases to cover the special areas of the Institute courses, which include Islamic and traditional geometry and design. The Library is collecting the theoretical texts of René Guenon, A.K. Coomaraswamy, Titus Burckhardt, Martin Lings, Seyyed Hossein Nasr and other writers concerned with traditional art and belief. It also possesses cassette tapes of lectures given to Friends of the Centre and the Temenos Academy.

Approximate numbers of books: The number of books in this field is still relatively small, although the collection has been enriched by the gift of the library of the late Issam El Said, comprising some 500 items on Islamic subjects.

The VITA (Visual Islamic and Traditional Arts) course, formerly at the Royal College of Art, forms part of the Institute and has a small separate book collection.

Access: Access is available by appointment to readers whose research needs cannot be satisfied elsewhere, but borrowing is limited to staff and students of the Institute.

■   ## Public Record Office

See under: RICHMOND: Public Record Office.

■   ## Royal Anthropological Institute Manuscript and Archive Collection

See under: LONDON: British Museum Ethnography Library.

Royal Asiatic Society Library   ■

Address:	The Library, Royal Asiatic Society, 60, Queen's Gardens, London W2 3AF
Tel:	0171 724 4741
Fax:	0171 706 4008

The Royal Asiatic Society was founded on 15th March 1823 by the noted scholar of Sanskrit, Henry Thomas Colebrooke. It is dedicated to a variety of activities connected with the Near and Middle East and Asia. The Society administers the Oriental Translation Fund (to facilitate publication of original translations of oriental texts) and the RAS Monograph Fund (to publish original work in the field of oriental studies).

Approximate numbers of books: The Library contains more than 100,000 volumes of books and periodicals dealing with various oriental languages, literatures, cultures and religions. No exact breakdown of these books by subject is currently available. The Library also possesses a unique collection of manuscripts.

Access: Access is primarily for Fellows of the Society but in special cases others may be admitted.

See: MWP p. 187, Pearson pp. 93, 173, 185, 303, 313, Roman pp. 27–28, Roper 3 pp. 497–500.

See also: The pamphlet issued by the Royal Asiatic Society entitled *The Royal Asiatic Society: Its Activities and Objectives*; O. Codrington, 'Catalogue of the Arabic, Persian, Hindustani and Turkish MSS in the Library of the Royal Asiatic Society'. The following work is essential reading for anyone interested in the Royal Asiatic Society and its library collections: Stuart Simmonds & Simon Digby (eds.), *The Royal Asiatic Society: Its History and Treasures*. This contains an excellent history of the Society by Professor C.F. Beckingham FBA.

Royal College of Art Library (Islamic Studies Section)   ■

See under: LONDON: Prince of Wales's Institute of Architecture Library.

■ Royal College of Physicians Library

Address:　The Library,
　　　　　　　Royal College of Physicians,
　　　　　　　11, St. Andrews Place,
　　　　　　　Regents Park,
　　　　　　　London NW1 4LE
Tel:　　　　0171 935 1174
Fax:　　　　0171 487 5218

Most of the small collection, as might be expected, deals with health or medicine. There are a number of oriental manuscripts (Arabic nos. 1–45, Persian nos. 46–62), the earliest of which were bequeathed in the 17th Century by John Selden. There are also about 25 oriental printed books.

Access: Access is limited to staff and members of the College and bona fide researchers.

See: MWP pp. 188–189, Pearson p. 313, Roper 3 p. 501.
See also: A.S. Tritton, 'Catalogue of Oriental Manuscripts in the Library of the Royal College of Physicians'.

■ Royal Commonwealth Society

See under: CAMBRIDGE: Royal Commonwealth Society Collections.

■ Royal Geographical Society Library

Address:　The Library,
　　　　　　　Royal Geographical Society,
　　　　　　　1, Kensington Gore,
　　　　　　　London SW7 2AR
Tel:　　　　0171 589 5466　.
Fax:　　　　0171 584 4447
e-mail:　　library@rgs.org
JANET:　　rgs@uk.ac.bbk.ge

The Library
The Library dates back to the foundation of the Society in 1830. For the first few decades most of the books were works of travel and

exploration, and this applied to books on the Middle East as well as to books on other parts of the world. The books in the Library on the Middle East are virtually all in European languages. Not only works of travel are collected now but also academic geography books, e.g. on physical geography, population, economic geography, cultural geography etc.

There is one noteworthy special collection: the Brown Collection on Morocco. This Collection contains about 340 books, mainly on Morocco, but also some on neighbouring North African countries (Algeria, Tunisia). The Collection, which was originally the property of Dr. Robert Brown (1842–1895), who played a prominent part in the affairs of the Society and who has an entry in the *Dictionary of National Biography*, was purchased by the Society after his death, in 1896. Most of the items in the Collection are of 19th Century date but a number are of earlier date. They are generally works of history and travel.

The Middle East Collection as a whole consists mainly of works of travel and description, history and all aspects of geography. There is a small number of books on early Arab and Muslim geography and geographical thought. The coverage here is Africa north of the Sahara, the Sahara itself, and Western Asia as far as Iran (excluding the former Soviet Asia). A number of the books deal with the Arab Gulf.

New Geographical Literature and Maps ceased publication in December 1980. This was a twice yearly publication issued from 1951–1980, listing all important accessions to the Library and Map Room over a six-month period. It listed works on the Middle East by name of country under the sections *Asia* and *Africa*.

Approximate numbers of books: The Middle East collection comprises about 4300 books, including those in the Brown Collection.

The Map and Atlas Collections
These are kept in the Society's Map Room. There is a good representative collection of maps of all regions of the Middle East (and of the world). It has not been possible to quantify the maps covering the Middle East.

The Royal Geographical Society (RGS) Archive Collections
These mainly comprise a collection of documents arising out of the Society's business since its foundation in 1830, i.e. papers relating

to expeditions which received the Society's help, correspondence with travellers, route notebooks, topographical and meteorological observations, MS maps, photographs and articles on travel submitted for publication in the Society's Journal. Some further documents have been deposited with the Society because they relate to persons and subjects of interest to the Society and these include some which are concerned with archaeological work in the Middle East and in the Sahara in the 19th and early 20th centuries. There are a dozen items which date from the late 18th and early years of the 19th centuries.

Approximate numbers of documents: There are about 300 notebooks, travel diaries and groups of documents concerned with the Middle East, approximately 20 from Egypt and the Sudan, approximately 50 from West Africa and the Sahara. There are also: notebooks and journals from Major D. Denham's expedition from Tripoli to Bornu (1821–1825), some notebooks of Sir Henry Rawlinson's from Mesopotamia (1843–1850), archaeological sketches in notebooks of Gertrude Bell, and a collection of the records made by Francis Rodd (Lord Rennell of Rodd) during his expedition to the Air Mountains (1922 and 1927). A very small number of documents deal with the Arab Gulf, e.g. a list of names of places on the Gulf in 1826 drawn up by R. Taylor, and a description of a voyage in the Gulf (1828–1829) by Edward Stirling.

The RGS Picture Library

The Picture Library provides a source of over half a million images, colour and black and white. Subject coverage comprises exploration and geographical activities and includes Middle Eastern imagery. The collection is available for commercial publishing and academic research.

Access: The Library and Archives, being supported entirely by Fellows' subscriptions, are open only to members of the Society. Archive materials are available for consultation on Library premises, by appointment only. The Picture Library is a commercial enterprise and therefore charges accordingly; it is open by appointment only. However, the Map Room is open to the general public without charge. The Library closes annually from mid-June to mid-July.

See: Jones p. 163, MWP pp. 190–195.

Royal Institute of International Affairs Library   ▪

Address:	The Library,
`	The Royal Institute of International Affairs,
	Chatham House,
	10, St. James's Square,
	London SW1Y 4LE
Tel:	0171 957 5700
Fax:	0171 957 5710
e-mail:	riialibrary@gn.apc.org

The Library provides information and documentation to support the aims and work of the Royal Institute of International Affairs (RIIA) and its membership. The integrated collection of books, reference works, statistical series, official publications, journals, newspapers and press cuttings covers a wide spectrum of foreign and international affairs since 1918, with particular emphasis on political, security and economic issues of the most recent 30–35 years. Material is acquired primarily in English, French, German and other European languages. There are no Arabic holdings.

Approximate numbers of books: Material dealing with the Middle East, the Arab world and Islam is integrated in the general holdings. Around 6500 volumes deal with these subjects (out of 140,000); 27 of the 400 current periodicals focus on these areas, as do a further 40 current serials.

Access: Access is primarily for staff and individual and corporate members of the Institute. Non-members carrying out research at post-graduate level are welcome to apply for a reader's ticket on payment of a fee. Prospective users should contact the Librarian by letter or phone, in advance.

See: Jones pp. 163–165, MWP pp. 195–199.

■ School of Oriental and African Studies Library

Address:	The Library,
	School of Oriental and African Studies,
	University of London,
	Thornhaugh Street,
	Russell Square,
	London WC1H 0XG
Tel:	0171 637 2388
Fax:	0171 323 6220
Telex:	262433 W 6876
e-mail:	pc7@soas.ac.uk or ps4@soas.ac.uk

The Library of the School of Oriental and African Studies constitutes one of the largest and most prestigious collections of oriental and African books in Britain. It was founded in 1917 and from small beginnings now contains over 800,000 volumes. The 1961 Hayter Report designated the Library as a 'National Lending Library' for oriental and African studies. It should be recognised, however, that despite the large number of rare printed books and manuscripts held, the Library is primarily intended to be a working collection for SOAS staff and students, and it is increasing at the rate of about 20,000 items per year.

In 1973 the Library moved into a purpose-built building attached to its old home, with room for about one million volumes. In 1994 it began to approach its capacity and some expansion took place. A further increase in its capacity is being planned. The collection is organised on an area studies basis, with a number of sections, of which the most significant for this Directory are the *Islamic Near and Middle East Section* and the *Ancient Near East, Semitics and Judaica Section*. The former covers Islam in general, the geographical area stretching from Muslim Spain to Yakutia, and the living languages of the Middle East, except for Hebrew. This is contained in the latter section, which also includes modern Israel/Palestine. Other sections which include significant amounts of material on Islam are the *Africa Section, South Asia Section*, and the *South East Asian and Pacific Section*. A series of pamphlets has been produced to help readers to understand the organisation of the Library in detail.

Middle East acquisitions are affected by participation in a number of co-operative arrangements. Under the MELCOM scheme the Library collects in greater depth publications in Arabic on North Africa, publications in Persian and on Iran, and publications in Turkish and on Turkey. Under the SCOLMA scheme the Library concentrates on European-language publications on North Africa.

Approximate numbers of books and manuscripts: (a) *Islamic Near and Middle East Section*: There are more than 75,000 items, including Arabic mss c.20; Persian mss c.400; Turkish mss 45; books dealing with the Near and Middle East written in European languages 12,000; on Islam more than 3000; on Central Asia more than 3000; and in the vernaculars of the area 35,000 in Arabic, 10,000 in Persian and 7000 in Turkish. (b) *Ancient Near East, Semitics and Judacia Section*: There are c.33,000 items including: Hebrew c.15,000; Yiddish c.3000; works on Israel, Hebraica and Judaica in Western languages c.7000; Ancient Near East c.8000. There is only a tiny number of Hebrew and Christian oriental manuscripts: Coptic 2; Ethiopic 8.

Access: Since 1989 all new acquisitions have been catalogued on an on-line system which is accessible via the internet. This includes nearly all serials and heavily used older items (for example, all items in the Teaching Collection). To be sure of accessing all the holdings of the Library, however, it is necessary to consult the card catalogues. Author, title and subject catalogues of *The SOAS, University of London, Library Catalogue* have been published by G.K. Hall of Boston (see Bibliography *sv School of Oriental and African Studies*). Membership of the Library is available to academic staff and students of British Universities. Other researchers may apply for external membership. For this a letter of recommendation is required, stating the reasons for needing to use the Library. A fee may be charged. Further details of external membership may be obtained from the Membership Desk.

See: Auch. pp. 71–77, MWP pp. 203–208, Pearson pp. 54, 117, 145, 172, 303, 312–313, Roman pp. 23–25, Roper 3 pp. 502–505.
See also: Adam Gacek, *Catalogue of the Arabic Manuscripts in the Library of the School of Oriental and African Studies*.

MASS: Iran, Israel, North Africa, Turkey.

■ School of Slavonic and East European Studies Library

Address:	School of Slavonic and East European Studies Library, University of London, Senate House, Malet Street, London WC1E 7HU
Tel:	0171 637 4934 ext. 4094
Fax:	0171 436 8916
e-mail:	ssees-library@ssees.ac.uk

The Library's area of interest includes the former Soviet Union and the Balkans. History, the Social Sciences and the Slavonic and East European languages and literatures are the principal subjects covered. Material is not collected in the local languages of the countries of the Caucasus and Central Asia that were formerly part of the Soviet Union but their history and culture are covered generally. The collection on the Balkan countries includes some material relating to Islamic culture and Turkish history.

Approximate numbers of books: former Soviet Central Asia (all aspects) c.1200 book titles; Balkan countries (Hungary, former Yugoslavia, Romania, Albania, Bulgaria – all aspects) c.59,000 volumes of books and pamphlets.

Access: Part of the Catalogue is available for access on the network: Telnet consull.ull.ac.uk (username SSEES).

Anyone studying in the Slavonic and East European field is welcome to use the Library. For a single visit no formality is required apart from signing the Visitors' Book. However, those who wish to use the Library over a period of time must complete an application form for a reader's ticket. In some cases a fee may be charged.

■ Science Reference and Information Service

See under: LONDON: The British Library.

Sion College Library   ■

Address: Sion College Library,
Victoria Embankment,
London EC4Y 0DN
Tel: 0171 353 7983

Sion College is a Society of Anglican clergymen which possesses one of the best theological libraries in Britain. It has about 100,000 volumes including many rare or unique works of theology. There is no separate collection dealing with Islam and the Middle East: the books in this subject area form part of the general collection, and constitute a very small part of the Library's holdings. The oriental manuscripts include items in Arabic, Persian and Turkish. There are also some Hebraic/Judaic printed books in the general collection.

Approximate numbers of books: Islam c.88 printed books; Arabic language c.25 printed books; Middle East history c.30 printed books; Oriental manuscripts 19; Hebrew manuscripts 3.

Access: Access is restricted to subscribing members of Sion College and bona fide enquirers *by prior appointment only.*

See: Roper 3 p. 505.

Society for Promoting Christian Knowledge Library   ■

Address: Archives and Library,
The Society for Promoting Christian Knowledge (SPCK),
Holy Trinity Church,
Marylebone Road,
London NW1 4DU
Tel: 0171 387 5282

The book collection is confined to file copies of SPCK publications from c.1830 to the present time. These include limited numbers of works on Islam, Middle East history and religious affairs (e.g. Archbishop's Mission to Assyrian Christians), and Arabic versions of the Scriptures, Book of Common Prayer and religious literature. The Society's archives contain detailed records of its production of the Arabic New Testament, the Psalter, and certain tracts during the third decade of the 18th Century, including a log of William

Caslon's employment in cutting a new fount of Arabic type and an original proof from it. Much information about translators, and the hazards, linguistic and doctrinal, of their work is to be found both in these early records and in the minute books of the SPCK's Foreign Translation Committee, set up in 1834 to supervise all foreign language publishing.

Access: Access is by appointment only.

See: Jones p. 165, MWP pp. 209–210.

■ Society of Antiquaries of London Library

Address:	The Library,
	Society of Antiquaries of London,
	Burlington House,
	Piccadilly,
	London W1V 0HS
Tel:	0171 734 0193/0171 437 9954
Fax:	0171 287 6967

The main subjects covered by the Library are archaeology (especially British), architectural history and the decorative arts (especially mediaeval), heraldry and older works on British local history and genealogy.

Approximate numbers of books: There are no special Middle Eastern collections but the Library has about 1000 books on the archaeology of the Near and Middle East with about 10 periodical titles.

Access: The Library can be used for reference and without appointment by Fellows and members of the Royal Archaeological Institute and the British Archaeological Association. Other readers may use the Library for a limited period on the recommendation of a Fellow or university tutor, or by arrangement with the Librarian or General Secretary. Visitors are requested to sign the Visitors' Book on arrival.

United Arab Emirates Embassy Resource Centre ■

Address: Resource Centre,
           United Arab Emirates Embassy,
           30, Prince's Gate,
           Knightsbridge,
           London SW7 1PT
Tel: 0171 581 1281
Fax: 0171 581 9616

The Library is now known as the Resource Centre. It is divided into two sections: (1) Information Centre, (2) Library. The Information Centre deals with enquiries from the public, in the form of telephone calls, letters, faxes and visitors. The enquiries are mainly about employment, living in the United Arab Emirates and tourism. There are also many general enquiries which may be categorised as miscellaneous. The Library contains books on the Emirates and the Middle East for lending and reference purposes. The majority of publications are in English. It is also possible to borrow photographs, slides, videos and flags. Newspapers and press cuttings are no longer retained.

Access: Students and members of the public may have access to the Library during normal working hours, usually by appointment.

United Society for the Propagation of the Gospel (USPG) Library ■

See under: LONDON: Partnership House Mission Studies Library
               OXFORD: USPG Archives, Rhodes House Library.

University College London Library ■

Address: The Library,
           University College London,
           Gower Street,
           London WC1E 6BT
Tel: 0171 380 7792/7793 (Main issue desk)
           0171 380 7795/7789
e-mail: library@ucl.ac.uk

The Middle Eastern collections of University College Library reflect the teaching and research interests of the College over the years in such subjects as Hebrew, Akkadian and Egyptology. Thus the Library possesses distinguished collections in the fields of Egyptology and Hebrew and Jewish Studies: the Mocatta Library of Anglo-Judaica was originally given to University College, London (UCL) in 1906 by the Jewish Historical Society of England, but much of it was destroyed in 1941. However, the Library was reformed and reopened in UCL in 1954. The letters and papers of Dr. Moses Gaster are housed in the Mocatta Library. In 1990 the Mocatta Library and UCL's Judaica collection were merged to form the Jewish Studies Library, which is housed in the Arnold Mishcon Reading Room in the Main Library at UCL. There is also the Edwards Library of Egyptology which is a departmental library situated away from the main library buildings (in the D.M.S. Watson Building, 1st floor), and to which a fine museum of Egyptian antiquities, containing the distinguished Edwards and Petrie Collections of Egyptian materials, is attached. The Edwards Library covers the whole history of Egypt up to Roman times and has much material on ancient Egyptian art and religion as well as many relevant periodicals.

The College Library has received many outstanding bequests over the years. In the Middle Eastern field two of the most notable have been: (a) the Egyptological Library of Sir Alan Gardiner (a President of the Egypt Exploration Society) which was presented in 1963 and contained over 1800 volumes not already possessed by the Edwards Library of Egyptology; and (b) the c.7000 volume Library of the former Chief Rabbi Sir Israel Brodie.

Approximate numbers of books: University College Library as a whole has over one million books, pamphlets and volumes of periodicals. No figures are available for the individual oriental collections.

Access: Access with borrowing rights is available to College staff and students, and others at the discretion of the Librarian.

See: See Jones pp. 216–217 (for Anglo-Jewish Archives), 223, MWP pp. 212–213, Pearson pp. 53–54, 313.
See also: University College, *The Gaster Papers*.

Victoria and Albert Museum Library   ■

See under: LONDON: National Art Library.

Warburg Institute Library   ■

Address: The Library,
The Warburg Institute,
University of London,
Woburn Square,
London WC1H 0AB
Tel: 0171 580 9663
Fax: 0171 436 2852

The primary purpose of the Warburg Institute is the study of the classical tradition. As part of this it concerns itself with the origins of civilisation in ancient Near Eastern and Mediterranean culture. There is no Islamic collection as such but the 250,000 books and offprints, and 1000 runs of periodicals include works on Egypt, Assyria, Babylonia, Middle East, Persia, Judaism, Islam; Arabic, Jewish and Babylonian astronomy and astrology; ancient Eastern and Islamic art and the history of Egyptology.

Approximate numbers of books: (titles): Egypt 650; Assyria/ Babylonia 400; Persia 250; Judaism 2800; Islam 560; Egyptian astronomy and astrology 50; Babylonian astronomy and astrology 100; Arabic astronomy and astrology 125; Jewish astronomy and astrology 75; Ancient Eastern art (general) 100 (there are several hundred more titles listed under the specific culture area); Islamic art 650; History of Egyptology 75.

Access: Access is open to ticket holders. Application forms for tickets may be obtained at the Reception Desk on arrival.

See also: The pamphlet *The Warburg Institute* (1995) for a fuller description of the Library; and J.B. Trapp, 'Arabic Studies in the Warburg Institute'.

■ Wellcome Institute for the History of Medicine Library

Address:	The Library,
	The Wellcome Institute for the History of Medicine,
	183, Euston Road,
	London NW1 2BE
Tel:	0171 611 8888 (Wellcome Building)
	0171 611 8582 (Library Enquiries)
Fax:	0171 611 8545
JANET:	uk.ac.ucl.wihm
Internet:	wihm.ucl.ac.uk

The Islamic and Near Eastern Collections form part of the important collection of oriental manuscripts and printed books acquired by Sir Henry Wellcome (1853–1936). This, together with his large collections of Western manuscripts, printed books and illustrative materials have, since his death, evolved into the present library of the Wellcome Institute for the History of Medicine supported by the Wellcome Trust. The Institute comprises an academic unit which provides courses for undergraduate and postgraduate students in association with University College London. A programme of symposia, seminars and lectures is also available to the general public. These facilities include courses and public lectures devoted to medical history in Islamic and Near Eastern cultures. The Library, one of the largest of its kind in the world, contains some 500,000 printed books dating from the 15th Century to the present, extensive collections of Western manuscripts, paintings and other iconographic materials as well as contemporary medical archives. Exhibitions are held which include Islamic materials from the collections and are occasionally focused on an Islamic theme.

Access (including Catalogue access): Persons wishing to consult or study any of the manuscripts or oriental printed books should apply in the first instance to the Curator of Oriental Manuscripts and Printed Books.

Most of the printed book collection and much of the iconographic collections are recorded in the Library's computerised database WILDCaT (Wellcome Institute Library Database) which is available through JANET and the Internet (for numbers see above). The Library provides the normal range of photographic facilities. A monthly accessions list is issued by the Library.

See: MWP pp. 214–220, Pearson pp. 145, 314–315, Roman pp. 25–27 Roper 3 pp. 507–509.

See also: [Approximate numbers of books and manuscripts are included in this section]:

(A) The following works, all produced by the Wellcome Institute, should be noted:
   - *Medical History*, the leading British journal on the subject, is published quarterly by the Institute and from time to time carries articles relevant to Islamic medicine and science.
   - *Current Work in the History of Medicine*, a quarterly bibliography, is also published by the Institute and includes items of Near Eastern interest.
   - *Wellcome Institute for the History of Medicine: A Brief Guide* (5th edn. 1993): A range of guides and booklets, of which this is one, relating to the Institute and its Library, have been published from time to time.

(B) The following works are useful as *general* introductions to the collections:
   - Nigel Allan, 'The Oriental Collections in the Wellcome Institute for the History of Medicine'.
   - S.A.J. Moorat, *Catalogue of Western Manuscripts on Medicine and Science in the Wellcome Historical Medical Library*.

(C) The following works describe (and enumerate) *specific* aspects of the oriental collections:
   - **Arabic**
     A.Z. Iskander, *A Catalogue of Arabic Manuscripts on Medicine and Science in the Wellcome Historical Medical Library*. In this Catalogue 197 manuscripts are described. The Library holds a further 800 Arabic manuscripts and 225 printed books.
   - **Armenian**
     V. Nersessian, 'Cuc'ak hayeren jer'agrec London Velk'om Institute gradarani' ['Catalogue of Armenian Manuscripts in the Wellcome Institute, London']. In this Catalogue 16 manuscripts are described including some Gospels with finely executed miniatures. There are, in addition, some manuscript fragments and 11 printed books.
   - **Coptic and Egyptian**
     S.G.J. Quirke & W.J. Tait, 'Egyptian manuscripts in the Wellcome Collection'. This describes Hieratic and Demotic papyri and five Coptic manuscripts. There is one Coptic printed book.

- **Ethiopian**
S. Strelcyn, 'Catalogue of Ethiopian Manuscripts of the Wellcome Institute of the History of Medicine in London'. 17 manuscripts are described. The Library holds a further five manuscripts, one printed book in Tigrinya and one in Amharic.
- **Hebrew**
N. Allan, 'Catalogue of Hebrew Manuscripts in the Wellcome Institute, London'; Idem., 'Catalogue of Hebrew Printed Books (1491–1900) in the Wellcome Institute, London'. The collection comprises 94 manuscripts, 58 of them Torah scrolls (some damaged), 162 Hebrew printed books and a further 28 in Yiddish.
- **Persian**
F. Keshavarz, *Descriptive and Analytical Catalogue of Persian Manuscripts in the Library of the Wellcome Institute for the History of Medicine.* 617 manuscripts are described in this Catalogue and the Library holds 80 printed books.
- **Syriac**
N. Allan, 'Syriac Fragments in the Wellcome Institute Library'. The Library holds a few ancient manuscript fragments and six printed books.
- **Turkish**
The Library holds a collection of 29 Ottoman manuscripts and 157 printed books.
- **Urdu**
S. Quraishi, 'Catalogue of Urdu, Panjabi and Kashmiri Manuscripts'. 19 Urdu manuscripts are described in the Catalogue. The Library holds c.130 printed books.

[Additionally, the Library holds two **Karshuni** manuscripts and one **Georgian** manuscript.]

■   Westminster University Library

See under: LONDON: Euston Centre Library, University of Westminster.

MANCHESTER

Central Library   ■

Address:	Central Library,
	St. Peter's Square,
	Manchester M2 5PD
Tel:	0161 234 1983 (Social Sciences Library)
Fax:	0161 234 1963 (Social Sciences Library)
Telex:	667149

The basic collection of books on Judaism was enlarged in 1949 by two gifts: one from the Moses Gaster Lodge of the Order of B'nai Brith and the other from the Israel Sunlight Library Committee. However, several years ago the Jewish Library ceased to exist as a separate entity within Manchester Libraries and Theatres, although most of its reference stock was retained and incorporated into the stock of the Social Sciences Library.

Access: Access to the collection may be gained through the Social Sciences Library but there is no longer a subject librarian in charge of it, nor does any member of staff in the Social Sciences Library have any particular knowledge of (or expertise in) the subjects it covers. The Library is open to members of the public.

See: Auch. pp. 62–63, Jones pp. 221–222, MWP p. 288.

Chetham's Library   ■

See under: MANCHESTER: John Rylands University Library of Manchester.

Jewish Library (Manchester Central Library)   ■

See under: MANCHESTER: Central Library.

■ John Rylands University Library of Manchester

Address: The John Rylands University Library of Manchester,
Oxford Road,
Manchester M13 9PP
Tel: 0161 275 3738
Fax: 0161 273 7488

Oriental languages have been studied at Manchester University since its foundation in 1851. Mrs. Rylands founded the private John Rylands Library to commemorate her husband's name, and it opened in 1900. In 1972 Manchester University Library and the John Rylands Library merged, to form the John Rylands University Library of Manchester.

One of the collections which Mrs. Rylands purchased for the John Rylands Library was the Althorp Library which belonged to the Earl Spencer. This contained the nucleus of the present Library's Oriental and Western manuscript collection. Other Arabic, Persian and Turkish manuscripts have been added as well as manuscripts and materials in Akkadian, Egyptian, Hebrew, Samaritan, Coptic, Ethiopian, Armenian and Pashto.

The Genizah fragments, formerly in Chetham's Library (at Long Millgate, Manchester M3 1SB, Tel: 0161 834 7961), have now been deposited on loan at the John Rylands University Library. The Library's Near Eastern Collection, started in 1948, has continued to grow and keep pace with the requirements of the Department of Middle Eastern Studies. Its core comprises literary texts and translations as well as modern works on Middle East and Maghribi history, traditional and Islamic sciences and philology. It should be noted that many of the books in Western languages on such subjects as Judaism, art, economics, anthropology etc. with reference to the Middle East, are to be found shelved in a variety of places in the library.

Approximate numbers of books: Arabic 18,500; Hebrew 6000; Persian 6700; Turkish 5900; Other Middle Eastern categories 34,500.

Access: Access to the Deansgate building is free to all bona fide students and researchers. Prior written application is normally required, although immediate admission may sometimes be possible on production of a letter of introduction and/or formal proof of identity. Access to the Main University Library on Oxford Road is available, for an annual charge. Library users who are not members of the University of Manchester may not borrow books from the Library.

See: Auch. pp. 56–63, MWP pp. 289–290, Pearson pp. 51, 59, 93–94, 117, 129, 144–145, 173, 303, 315–316, Roman pp. 40–42, Roper 3 pp. 509–512. **See also:** A. Mingana, *Catalogue of the Arabic Manuscripts in the John Rylands Library, Manchester*; C.E. Bosworth, A.S. Radwan & S.A.M. Sa'id, *A Catalogue of Accessions to the Arabic Manuscripts in the John Rylands University Library of Manchester*; F. Taylor, 'The Oriental Manuscript Collections in the John Rylands Library'; Stefan Strelcyn, *Catalogue of Ethiopic Manuscripts in the John Rylands University Library of Manchester*; for details of other published catalogues of the Library's Middle Eastern Language manuscripts, see the invaluable guide by Dr. David Brady (esp. pp. 16–17) entitled *Middle Eastern and Judaic Studies: A Guide to Research Resources*, (Manchester: John Rylands Library & Department of Middle Eastern Studies, 1995).

NEWCASTLE UPON TYNE

■ Newcastle upon Tyne University Library

See under: NEWCASTLE UPON TYNE: The Robinson Library, University of Newcastle upon Tyne.

■ The Robinson Library, University of Newcastle upon Tyne

Address:	The Robinson Library,
	University of Newcastle,
	Newcastle upon Tyne NE2 4HQ
Tel:	0191 222 6000/7587
Fax:	0191 222 6235
Telex:	53654 (UNINEW G)
e-mail:	ian.mowat@newcastle.ac.uk

There are a small number of books on Islam and the Middle East, chosen by the Religious Studies, Politics and History Departments of the University over the years. The Library also possesses, however, a much more important collection, the Gertrude Bell Archive. This comprises the papers, books, photographs, letters and travel diaries of the famous traveller and Middle Eastern explorer Gertrude Margaret Lowthian Bell (1868–1926). The papers and books are conserved by the Robinson Library while the photographs are in the care of the University's Department of Archaeology. In Lesley Gordon's booklet, *Gertrude Bell*, (written to accompany the British Council/University of Newcastle exhibition *Gertrude Bell*, which opened in the Central Library, Newcastle upon Tyne, on 11 July 1994), the Archive is described as follows: 'The material consists largely of books on Near and Middle Eastern language, literature, history, art, archaeology and architecture, and it came with a collection of some 6000 photographs, many contained in albums, as well as negatives and slides. The pictures are largely of Eastern scenes, often of archaeological sites, some of which, with the passage of years, have substantially changed or have disappeared altogether. There are also a number, of considerable ethnological and anthropological interest, of the tribal peoples. This collection [having been deposited at Armstrong College in 1926] was supplemented some sixty years later, and as a result of the kind agreement of the then Cleveland County Librarian and his Committee, by the deposit on permanent loan of four albums of photographs of Gertrude Bell's 1903 round-the-world tour, which were discovered at the Redcar branch of Cleveland County Library.'

In 1962 the University of Newcastle received a further gift, which comprised some 1600 of Gertrude's letters, together with her diaries and a number of other items. In 1965 the University was given part of Gertrude Bell's correspondence with Charles Doughty-Wylie, and in 1982 the Middle East Centre of St. Antony's College, Oxford 'donated the diary of the Hayil journey Gertrude kept for Doughty-Wylie, together with some further letters to him'. The photographs and papers in the Archive have been conserved and a set of copy prints and copy negatives exists. Approximate numbers of books: Middle East and Islam c.3000 (of which c.2000 volumes belong to the Gertrude Bell Collection).

Access: Access to the main Library is freely available for staff and students of the University. Other persons may be admitted at the discretion of the Librarian. Access to the Gertrude Bell Archive, including the photographs and papers, is by appointment only. The text of Bell's letters and diaries has been made much more accessible to the general public as a result of the work of Lynn Ritchie, a University Research Associate, who, between 1982 and 1988 transcribed the text: the transcripts, with their indices, may be consulted in the Robinson Library, and are available in hard copy form as well as being on computer.

See: Jones p. 223, MWP p. 295.
See also: Winifred Cotterill Donkin, *Catalogue of the Gertrude Bell Collection in the Library of King's College, Newcastle upon Tyne.* [out of print]. A catalogue of the papers was produced by the University Library in 1966, and a catalogue of the photographs appeared from the University Department of Archaeology in 1982 (2nd edn. 1985).

NOTTINGHAM

■   Nottingham University Library

Address:	Nottingham University Library,
	Hallward Library,
	University Park,
	Nottingham NG7 2RD
Tel:	0115 951 4548
Fax:	0115 951 4558
e-mail:	uazmain@vme.ccc.nottingham.ac.uk
JANET:	uk.ac.nottingham.library
Telnet:	library.nott.ac.uk

Approximate numbers of books: Islam 550; Judaica 700; History of the Middle East 650.

The Manuscripts Department of the Library possesses a few Islamic manuscripts which are in the Parkyns of Bunny (Notts) Collection.

Access: Enquiries about access to the Main Library and the Manuscripts Department should be addressed to the Librarian.

See: MWP pp. 297–300, Roper 3 p. 513.

OXFORD

All Souls College Library ■

See under: OXFORD: Codrington Library.

Ashmolean Museum Eastern Art Library ■

See under: OXFORD: Bodleian Library
OXFORD: Oriental Institute Library.

Balfour Library (Pitt Rivers Museum) ■

Address:	Balfour Library,
	Pitt Rivers Museum,
	South Parks Road,
	Oxford OX1 3PP
Tel:	01865 270926
Fax:	01865 270943

The Balfour Library has been built up to illustrate and explain the subject interests of the Pitt Rivers Museum, namely ethnology, anthropology, prehistoric archaeology, music, religion and pre-industrial technology. It is named after Henry Balfour, first curator of the Museum, who left his personal library to the Museum on his death in 1939; the collection formed the core of the Library. The Library now has the dual function of being the research library of the Museum and representing the full range of teaching interests of the School of Anthropology. Although the Library is not specifically concerned with the Middle East and the Islamic world, the collection includes a small holding on these areas. The sizeable collection of general and theoretical monographs and periodicals on ethnology and archaeology contains much of interest to the Middle Eastern specialist. The Museum archives also have a small collection of photographs of the Middle East from the late 19th and early 20th Centuries, which include such areas as Islamic North Africa and the Sudan. There is also a small collection of manuscripts of anthropological interest, particularly on North Africa, including a collection of manuscript and typescript material from M.W. Hilton-Simpson relating particularly to Berber medicine (1914–1926).

Approximate numbers of books: c.500 books dealing with the Middle East, the Arab Gulf and the Islamic world on the subjects mentioned above.

Access: The Library may be used by members of the University of Oxford. Other persons may be admitted at the discretion of the Librarian. Archive collections are available by appointment only, through the Assistant Curator (Archives) in the first instance.

See: Morgan p. 182, MWP p. 323, Pearson p. 309, Roper 3 pp. 522–523.

■ Bodleian Library

Address:	The Bodleian Library,
	Broad Street,
	Oxford OX1 3BG
Tel:	01865 277000
	01865 277180 (Admissions Office)
	01865 277034 (Dept. of Oriental Books Reading Room)
	01865 277033 (Keeper of Oriental Books)
	01865 277017 (Keeper of Printed Books)
Fax:	01865 277182
	01865 277029 (Dept. of Oriental Books)
Telex:	83656
e-mail:	adrian.roberts@bodley.ox.ac.uk

The Bodleian Library was founded in 1598 and opened to the public in 1602. The founder, Sir Thomas Bodley (1545–1613), was himself a competent Hebraist, and from its inception the Library has acquired materials for oriental studies. Prominent among these are the magnificent collections of manuscripts which entered the Library in the 17th and early 18th Centuries. A high proportion are Arabic, among them some of the Library's most precious treasures. Persian manuscripts are also represented but the richness of the present collection owes much to the accessions of the 19th Century. Most of the Bodleian's Indian and Persian miniatures were acquired at that time. The Turkish holdings, though added to in recent years, are smaller and in general less distinguished. Manuscripts in Malay, Urdu and a number of minor languages are also to be found in the Library. Among the College manuscripts on deposit in the Library are a number of items of Islamic interest.

The development of the Bodleian Library coincided with the expansion of serious oriental studies in the 17th Century, and this circumstance is reflected in the substantial holdings of printed works by early English and continental orientalists. Today, the Library receives books and periodicals in European languages on most aspects of the history and culture of the Islamic world. Its status as a library of copyright deposit ensures comprehensive coverage of United Kingdom publications. In addition, the store of Arabic, Persian and Turkish printed material is continually added to. Emphasis is placed on the traditional branches of learning (supplementing the manuscript collections), but the works of established modern writers are not neglected.

Secondary works in European languages on Islam in South Asia, as well as a small number of Urdu publications, are acquired by the Indian Institute Library, a 'Dependent' library within the Bodleian administration. It also holds some older collections of printed books in Arabic and Persian. Rhodes House Library (*qv*), another 'Dependent' library, acquires non-vernacular works on the Islamic countries of the Commonwealth (excluding South Asia) and sub-Saharan Africa.

Care of the Bodleian's Islamic material rests largely with the Department of Oriental Books. The Department, which was set up in 1931, has charge of manuscripts in all oriental languages, as well as printed books wholly or substantially in oriental languages (excluding those of India, Pakistan and Bangladesh). Works in European languages of oriental interest, including Islamic studies, are divided according to subject between the Department of Oriental Books and the Department of Printed Books. Broadly speaking, only works on oriental languages and their literatures are assigned to the former Department.

Approximate numbers of books and manuscripts: Islamic materials in European languages are scattered throughout the Library, arranged according to several successive methods of classification or embedded in the 'named' collections. The compilation of statistics would be a long and involved under-taking, and for the present remains impracticable. There are no subject catalogues. Manuscripts and printed books in the care of the Department of Oriental Books are not classified by subject, but the following tentative figures are offered for the more important language categories:

Manuscripts
- **Arabic:** 2350 (excluding papyri but including Christian Arabic manuscripts – some 300 counting Karshuni and bilingual Coptic-Arabic texts)
- **Persian:** 2530
- **Turkish:** 480
- **Hebrew** 3000
- **Urdu:** 75
- **Malay:** 20

Printed Books (approximate nos. of titles as of March 1995)
- **Arabic:** 14,000
- **Persian:** 6000
- **Turkish:** 17,000
- **Hebrew:** 24,000 [The figure of 40,000 given in Netton, *Middle East Materials* (1983), p. 104 was wildly wrong!]
- **Malay/Indonesian:** 750
- **Kurdish:** 225

The following points should be noted in connection with the above figures for printed books:

(a) The figures represent titles not volumes and include serials.
(b) As well as publications wholly or substantially in the languages concerned, the figures include translations from those languages, and European language works on the linguistics and literatures of those languages.
(c) 'Persian' covers not only New Persian (and Tadjik) but also all dialects of Old and Middle Persian.
(d) 'Turkish', besides Ottoman and the language of the Turkish Republic, embraces the other languages of the Turkic group.
(e) The figures for Hebrew exclude Judaica, which are part of the Library's general holdings and cannot be quantified at present, but include books in Yiddish.

Access (including Catalogue access): Cataloguing on the Online Public Access Catalogue began in September 1988. This includes acquisitions in oriental languages (other than Chinese and Japanese). Of the two sections of the Library's General Catalogue, the Pre-1920 Catalogue is available on CD-ROM, and work is in progress on the retrospective conversion of the

Post-1920 Catalogue. For works in Near Eastern languages acquired before 1989 the card catalogue in the Reading Room of the Department of Oriental Books should be consulted. From most Reading Rooms, including that of the Department of Oriental Books, the Library provides access to a large number of networked databases.

Only persons formally admitted as readers may enter and use the Library. There is normally no access to the bookstacks and no book may be borrowed. (Under the inter-library loan scheme certain categories of books may be lent to other libraries for consultation there.) Serious researchers are welcome provided that adequate notice of their visit and means of identification are given. Certain select manuscripts are issued only at the discretion of the Keeper of Oriental Books, to whom written application must be made.

See: Auch. pp. 64–70, Jones p. 217, MWP pp. 300–313, Pearson pp. 55–57, 90–91, 116, 172, 185, 199, 303, 307–308, 313, Roman pp. 29–34, Roper 3 pp. 513–519.

See also: A.F.L. Beeston, 'The Oriental Manuscript Collections of the Bodleian Library'; A.E. Cowley, *A Concise Catalogue of the Hebrew Printed Books in the Bodleian Library*; A. Neubauer, *A Catalogue of the Hebrew Manuscripts in the Bodleian Library and in the College Libraries of Oxford.*

See also under: OXFORD: Jesus College Library

OXFORD: Oriental Institute Library.

Christis Church Library

Address:	The Library,
	Christ Church,
	Oxford OX1 1DP
Tel:	01865 276169

The Library holds about fifty relevant manuscripts, the overwhelming majority of which are in Hebrew or Arabic. Since the compilation of the Latin catalogue listed below, the principal item of interest to be added to the collection has been an early 17th Century manuscript of Jalal al-Din Rumi, given by the Rev. Cuthbert King, formerly of the ICS, in 1972. The Library also has a collection of some 1750 books, partly in Hebrew, in the Morris Library, which stems from the personal library of Dr. John Morris, the 17th Century Professor of Hebrew: this is of considerable interest for the development of Hebrew in Oxford.

Access: Access is available to members of Christ Church College, and bona fide research scholars by prior arrangement.

See: Morgan pp. 24–34, MWP pp. 319–320, Pearson pp. 56, 309, Roper 3 pp. 519–520.
See also: G.W. Kitchin, *Catalogus codicum mss qui in Bibliotheca Aedis Christi apud Oxonienses adservantur.*

■ Codrington Library, All Souls College

Address:	Codrington Library, All Souls College, Oxford OX1 4AL
Tel:	01865 279318
Fax:	01865 279299

The Library does not collect material relating to the Middle East and has no modern collection on the subject. However, it does hold a number of 18th Century Persian manuscripts. These have rarely been studied and there is no recent catalogue of them.

Access: Access is by appointment only.

See: Roman p. 34, Roper 3 p. 514.

■ Institute of Agricultural Economics Library

See under: OXFORD: International Development Centre Library, Queen Elizabeth House.

■ Institute of Commonwealth Studies Library

See under: OXFORD: International Development Centre Library, Queen Elizabeth House.

■ Institute of Social and Cultural Anthropology Library

See under: OXFORD: Tylor Library, Institute of Social and Cultural Anthropology.

International Development Centre Library, Queen Elizabeth House

Address:	International Development Centre Library,
	Queen Elizabeth House,
	21 St. Giles,
	Oxford OX1 3LA
Tel:	01865 273590
Fax:	01865 273607
e-mail:	qehlib@sable.ox.ac.uk

The International Development Centre Library was established in 1989 by the merger of two formerly independent libraries: the Library of the Institute of Commonwealth Studies and the Library of the Institute of Agricultural Economics. The subject areas covered are: development, finance, aid, trade, commodities, economic aspects of agriculture, human resources and sustainable development. The emphasis is on 'Third World' or 'old' developing countries, and this includes some material on the Middle East.

Access (including Catalogue access): The Catalogue is available on the Internet, either through the Oxford University Information System, or directly through the Library Home Page (http://info.ox.ac.uk:80/~qehlib). Borrowing facilities are available to members of Oxford University; others may use the Library for reference. Advance notice of visitors is appreciated.

Jesus College Library

Address:	The Library,
	Jesus College,
	Oxford OX1 3DW
Tel:	01865 279700
Fax:	01865 279687 (marked for the attention of the Librarian or the Archivist)
e-mail:	library@jesus.ox.ac.uk

The College does not have anything which could be termed an Islamic or Middle Eastern Collection. However, among the collection of books relating to former members of College, there is a far from complete collection of works by T.E. Lawrence, or relating to him; this collection is kept in the Fellows' Library. It includes Lawrence's own copy of C.M. Doughty's *Arabia Deserta*, in the two-volume edition of 1921 with an introduction by Lawrence. The College's remains of Lawrence also include the original typescript of his 1910 undergraduate dissertation, 'The Influence of the Crusades on European Military Architecture – to the End of the XIIth Century', and a collection of letters from him to Colonel R.V. Buxton and others dating from the years 1922–1935.

The College's older manuscripts are, for the most part, deposited in the Bodleian Library (*qv*). They include: a fragment of the Qur'an dating perhaps from the 16th Century (Ms 24); a Qur'an (Ms 117), also perhaps from the same century, given by the Rev. David Jones in 1744, sent to him from Aleppo in 1710; and an Arabic–Latin dictionary compiled by the Rev. David Jones in 1691 (Ms 120). (The numbering of these manuscripts is taken from the Jesus College section of Volume 2 of Coxe's volume listed below, which contains fuller descriptions of the manuscripts in question. A copy of the Catalogue is to be found in the Bodleian Library.)

Access: The Library is not normally open to members of the public. Bona fide scholars wishing to consult materials should apply in writing to the College Librarian or the Archivist, as appropriate. For access to the Bodleian Library, see the entry OXFORD: Bodleian Library.

See: Morgan pp. 48–52, MWP p. 322, Pearson pp. 56, 308
See also: H.O. Coxe, *Catalogus codicum mss qui in Collegiis aulisque Oxoniensibus hodie adservantur.*

■   ## Kressel Collection

See under: OXFORD: Leopold Muller Memorial Library (Oxford Centre for Hebrew and Jewish Studies).

■   ## Leopold Muller Memorial Library
(Oxford Centre for Hebrew and Jewish Studies)

Address:	The Leopold Muller Memorial Library,
	Oxford Centre for Hebrew and Jewish Studies,
	Yarnton Manor,
	Yarnton,
	Oxford OX5 1PY
Tel:	01865 377946
Fax:	01865 375079

The Leopold Muller Memorial Library is made up in the main of two private collections. The Kressel Collection has been at Yarnton since 1974 and covers mainly Jewish history and Jewish literature of the last two centuries. The majority of the material is in Hebrew. The Elkoshi Collection, which has not yet been catalogued, consists of 17,000 volumes of modern Hebrew literature. These two collections have been augmented by the acquisition of several thousand books, mainly in English, and the Library is now divided into the following sections: Israel; History of Israel; History of the Jewish People; Holocaust; Zionism; Hebrew literature; Bible; Judaism; Biography; Periodicals; Reference Works; Bibliography. The Kressel Archive contains some 200,000 newspaper cuttings taken from the Hebrew press of the past hundred years, as well as newspapers, pamphlets and manuscripts.

Approximate numbers of books: the Library contains about 45,000 volumes, including the Elkoshi Collection.

Access: Access to the Collections is granted to all bona fide scholars.

See: Jones pp. 223–224.

MASS: Israel.

Lincoln College Library   ■

Address:	The Library,
	Lincoln College,
	Oxford OX1 3DR
Tel:	01865 279831

One of the most important bequests received by Lincoln College was that of Thomas Marshall (1621–1685) who was Rector of the College from 1672 until his death. This included many works in Hebrew and Arabic. Further details of this bequest appear in Green and Morgan listed below. Of particular note among the Hebrew items in the College Library are: *Zohar*, Cremona, 1519; Maimonides, *Mishnah Torah*, Venice 1574–1576; and Joseph Caro, *Beth Yosef*, 1550.

Approximate numbers of books: Hebrew language, Torah and Commentary c.200.

Access: Access to this collection is by written request only.

See: Morgan pp. 62–63, Pearson p. 56.
See also: V.H.H. Green, *The Commonwealth of Lincoln College 1427–1977.*

■ McGowin Library, Pembroke College

Address: McGowin Library,
        Pembroke College,
        Oxford OX1 1DW
Tel: 01865 276409
Fax: 01865 276418

The College Library is an undergraduate library and supports all undergraduate courses taught in the University of Oxford, (including Oriental Studies), but it is available to postgraduates if there is material which they wish to consult.

Approximate numbers of books and manuscripts: The Arabic collection consists of c.3000 volumes covering language, literature, history etc. and there is an annual budget for further purchase. There are also 17 Syriac religious manuscripts dating from 1193 to 1812, collected by an Old Member of the College and donated to the Library.

Access: Access is available to non-College members by appointment only.

■ Middle East Centre Library, St. Antony's College

Address: Middle East Centre Library,
        St. Antony's College,
        Woodstock Road,
        Oxford OX2 6JF
Tel: 01865 284764
Fax: 01865 311475
e-mail: derek.hopwood@sant.ox.ac.uk

The Library was established in 1955 as part of St. Antony's College, an institution which admits graduate students to the University of Oxford. The Library specialises in the study of the modern Middle East and covers history, economics, politics, Arabic literature, sociology and religion.

The collection includes books, periodicals, newspapers (in print and on microfilm), pamphlets, official publications and a large archive of the private papers, mostly unpublished, of diplomats, businessmen and others who worked in the Middle East. The area of study includes the Arabic speaking countries of the Middle East and North Africa plus Iran, Turkey and Israel.

Approximate numbers of books: There are approximately 33,000 volumes, excluding journals.

Access: All students and senior members of Oxford University and anyone from other universities with an adequate introduction may have access to the Library. Only senior members and graduate students of Oxford University may borrow.

See: Auch. pp. 64–70, Jones p. 222, Morgan p. 116–117, MWP pp. 323–332, Roman p. 34.
See also: Diana Grimwood-Jones (ed.), *Sources for the History of the British in the Middle East 1800–1978. A Catalogue of the Private Papers Collection in the Middle East Centre, St. Antony's College, Oxford.*

MASS: Iran, Israel, Jordan. Lebanon, Libya.

New College Library

Address:	The Library,
	New College,
	Oxford OX1 3BN
Tel:	01865 279580

There is a small collection of books on Arabic language and literature and other languages influenced by Islamic culture, which runs to approximately 50 items. (These are to be found on the ground floor in the language general reference section under G.R. 13 . . . and also in the basement stacks under G.G. . . .) In the history section on the ground floor (K. 3786ff) there are about 90 items on topics concerning Turkey, Iraq, Iran, Egypt, Israel and the Gulf States.

Access: Access and borrowing is limited to members of New College.

See: Roper 3 p. 522.

Oriental Institute Library

Address:	Oriental Institute Library,
	Pusey Lane,
	Oxford OX1 2LE
Tel:	01865 278202
Fax:	01865 278190
e-mail:	library@orinst.ox.ac.uk

The Islamic Collection forms a considerable part of the Oriental Institute Library's holdings. The Library was created in 1961 from a number of private specialised collections, the nuclei of which were often the private libraries of past professors: in the field of Arabic Studies that of Margoliouth is notable. The Library is primarily intended to meet the needs of the Faculty of Oriental Studies' teaching staff and students, and, in general, the holdings are strongest in those fields where examined courses are offered, i.e. language, literature, history, philosophy and culture *but* excluding (1) the more specialised areas of science and technology and (2) modern Arabic literature together with the contemporary history, politics, economics etc. of the Middle East and North Africa (with which the Middle East Centre Library, St. Antony's College, *qv*, is concerned). The Hebrew section of the Edersheim Collection, belonging to Exeter College, is on permanent loan to the Library.

The Oriental Institute Library has also administered, since 1971, the Eastern Art Library in the Ashmolean Museum, which is primarily the working library for staff of the Department of Eastern Art; its comprehensive coverage includes all aspects of the art and archaeology of the post-Islamic Near East. The books are for reference only. In 1993 all collections became a dependent library of the Bodleian.

Approximate numbers of books: Islam (including philosophy, Qur'an, hadith, fiqh) 3150; History 4200; Arabic language and literature 2850; Persian language and literature 2100; Turkish language and literature 2550; Hebrew language and literature 2200; Jewish and Biblical Studies Collection (including Biblical, Rabbinical and historical works as well as the last figure for Hebrew language and literature) 10,000; relevant periodicals taken 20. There are no manuscripts but there is a collection of pamphlets. The Islamic sections of the Eastern Art Library in the Ashmolean have about 2300 volumes.

Access: The Islamic collection is an open access collection. The Institute Library as a whole is open to all accredited readers of the Bodleian Library (*qv*); borrowing rights are given to current members of the University of Oxford and to others at the discretion of the Librarian. The Eastern Art Library may be used by accredited readers of the Bodleian; direct access is confined to staff of the Department of Eastern Art of the Ashmolean

Museum and the Oriental Institute, and to others with a recommendation from a member of the Department of Eastern Art or with the permission of the Librarian. The Edersheim Collection in the Oriental Institute Library is kept separately from the Jewish and Biblical Studies Collection and is not on open access or borrowable.

See: Auch. pp. 64–70, Morgan p. 42, Roman p. 34.

Oxford Centre for Hebrew and Jewish Studies Library   ■

See under: OXFORD: Leopold Muller Memorial Library (Oxford Centre for Hebrew and Jewish Studies).

Pembroke College Library   ■

See under: OXFORD: McGowin Library, Pembroke College.

Pitt Rivers Museum   ■

See under: OXFORD: Balfour Library (Pitt Rivers Museum).

Queen Elizabeth House Library   ■

See under: OXFORD: International Development Centre Library, Queen Elizabeth House.

Rhodes House Library   ■

Address: Rhodes House Library,
             South Parks Road,
             Oxford OX1 3RG
Tel: 01865 270909

Rhodes House Library deals with the history, current affairs and social sciences of the Commonwealth, Africa and the United States. The works which it possesses on the Middle East deal with Cyprus and with British administration in Palestine, Iraq and Aden.

Approximate numbers of books: History and administration: c.600, of which about 250 deal with Cyprus.

Access: Access to the Library is available to members of the University of Oxford, or those with a special need to use the Library who can present an appropriate letter of introduction.

See: Jones p. 224, MWP pp. 313–317.
See also under: OXFORD: USPG Archives, Rhodes House Library
LONDON: Partnership House Mission Studies Library.

■ St. Antony's College Library

See under: OXFORD: Middle East Centre Library, St. Antony's College

■ St. John's College Library

Address:	The Library,
	St. John's College,
	St. Giles',
	Oxford OX1 3JP
Tel:	01865 277330
Telex:	01865 277435 (not in Library)
e-mail:	library@fyfield.sjc.ox.ac.uk

The Library owns a number of manuscripts in Arabic, mostly through the gift of Archbishop Laud who founded the Chair of Arabic in the University. A catalogue of mss is in preparation. Otherwise the Library holds a small working collection supporting teaching in the Oriental Studies Final Honours School at Oxford.

Access: Admission is strictly by prior written appointment with the Librarian. During Vacations, prospective users are asked to allow for absence of the Librarian on leave etc. when writing for appointments.

See: Roman p. 34, Roper 3 pp. 523–524.
See also: H.O. Coxe, *Catalogus codicum mss qui in Collegiis aulisque Oxoniensibus hodie adservantur*, and supplements by H.M. Colvin.

Tylor Library, Institute of Social and Cultural Anthropology ∎

Address: Tylor Library,
Institute of Social and Cultural Anthropology,
51, Banbury Road,
Oxford OX2 6PE
Tel: 01865 274671
Fax: 01865 274630
e-mail: libisca@ox.ac.uk

The Library holds over 900 volumes on various aspects and areas of the Middle East, in addition to other titles on Islam in the wider world and numerous pamphlets. Items acquired from 1992 onwards, and some older holdings, are catalogued on OLIS.

Access: The Library is open to members of the University and bona fide visitors; a fee is payable for prolonged use by external readers.

See: Roper 3 pp. 520–521.

USPG Archives, Rhodes House Library ∎

Address: Rhodes House Library,
(Archives)   South Parks Road,
Oxford OX1 3RG
(1701–1965 approx.)
Tel: 01865 270909
Fax: 01865 270912
Enquiries: The Archivist
Address: Partnership House,
(Society)   157, Waterloo Road,
London SE1 8XA
Tel: 0171 837 4299
Fax: 0171 837 2371

In 1987 the United Society for the Propagation of the Gospel (USPG) moved from Tufton Street to a building in Waterloo Road, London, which it shares with the Church Missionary Society, called Partnership House. Part of the USPG Library therefore went towards the formation of a joint library, the Partnership House Mission Studies Library (*qv*). The major part of the USPG's Archive and the historical core of the Library, which were not required in London, were deposited on loan at Rhodes House Library (*qv*) in Oxford, a dependent library of the Bodleian Library (*qv*).

The USPG was formed in 1965 by the amalgamation of the Society for the Propagation of the Gospel in Foreign Parts (SPG), which had been founded in 1701, and the Universities Mission to Central Africa (UMCA), which had been founded in 1859. They were joined in 1968 by the Cambridge Mission to Delhi (CMD). Each Society had worked in areas where the influence of Islam was present and the USPG continues to do so to the present day. The SPG had been active throughout the world over its 250 years history, contact with Islam being encountered in the Indian sub-continent, South East Asia and West Africa. The Society's work in the Middle East was more limited. The UMCA encounter with Islam was in East Africa, on the Island of Zanzibar and in Tanzania. Important aspects of all three missionary societies' activities was the 'zenana' work of the women missionaries and the emphasis on education for both sexes.

The USPG Archive, covering the period from 1701 to approximately 1965, contains minutes, correspondence, annual reports, individual missionaries' reports and other records relating to all areas where the Societies worked. Of particular interest on the Middle East are records of the Crimea Memorial Church in Istanbul and correspondence with the Diocese of Jerusalem. The USPG pamphlet collection includes items on the Middle East and of wider interest.

The USPG's collection of books from its closed Library contains volumes on the Middle East, other areas of the Societies' work and on Islam. These are fairly inaccessible, and likely to remain so for some time: specific requests should be submitted to the Rhodes House Library Archivist to ensure relevant books are available.

Personal information about the Societies' missionaries is retained in London, so specific enquiries regarding missionaries should be directed to the Archivist at Partnership House. More recent records also remain in London and will be released to the public after thirty years.

Access: Access to the Archives held in Rhodes House Library may be obtained on application to the Archivist in advance. Admission is subject to Bodleian Library procedures since this is the parent institution.

Wadham College Library ■

Address:	The Library,
	Wadham College,
	Oxford OX1 3PN
Tel:	01865 277900

The Iranian section of the Library has books on most aspects of Iran's history and culture, but it specialises in history and literature from the beginning of the Islamic period up to the First World War. There is also a collection of Arabic and Persian manuscripts and lithographs, mainly consisting of Shi'i *fiqh* and theology, and a collection of Armenian printed books.

Approximate numbers of Books: Islam 420; Persian literature 700; Persian history 1500; Manuscripts 770; Lithographs 390; Armenian printed books 900.

Access: The Librarian's permission is necessary before the Library may be used.

See: Morgan pp. 146–150, Pearson pp. 172, 308–309, Roman p. 34, Roper 3 pp. 524–525.

PLYMOUTH

■   ## Plymouth Central Library

Address:	Central Library,
	Drake Circus,
	Plymouth PL4 8AL
Tel:	01752 385912 (Lending Library)
	01752 385907/385908
Fax:	01752 385929/385905

The Library includes the Holcenberg Foundation: this is a collection of books on the Bible, history of Jewry, biographies of famous Jewish people, sociological works, anti-Semitism and the Holocaust, Jewish humour and fiction, customs, cookery, modern Israel, and music. It was begun in 1962 and now amounts to more than 250 titles. Books and music are integrated with normal lending, reference and children's stock but a printed catalogue, updated annually, is available on request.

Access: The Library is open to all members of the public.

See: MWP pp. 332–333.

PORTSMOUTH

Frewen Library, University of Portsmouth   ■

Address:	Frewen Library,
	University of Portsmouth,
	Cambridge Road,
	Portsmouth PO1 2ST
Tel:	01705 876543
Fax:	01705 843233
e-mail:	library@uk.ac.port.csovax

An analysis of the relevant material reveals a handful of some 20 books on Arabic language. In addition, a search of the classified catalogue in conjunction with the subject index reveals that the Library has about a further 30–40 books dealing with Islamic topics.

Access: Access is particularly for staff and students at the University of Portsmouth. Visitors may either use the Library just for reference *or* register as *external* readers for a fee. This entitles them to borrow four books.

Portsmouth University Library   ■

See under: PORTSMOUTH: Frewen Library, University of Portsmouth.

RICHMOND

■   ## The Public Record Office

Address: Public Record Office,
Ruskin Avenue,
Kew, Richmond,
Surrey TW9 4DU
Tel: 0181 876 3444
Fax: 0181 878 8905

As might be expected, the Public Record Office (PRO) contains a large quantity of documentary material on the Middle East and other Islamic countries which were either part of the British Empire or had British diplomatic representation. Middle East material is fully listed and documented in over 26 pages of MWP (see below), which should be consulted by all interested readers. The PRO collections were formerly to be found both in the Kew and Chancery Lane buildings, but by January 1997 it is anticipated that all Chancery Lane material will have been transferred to Kew.

Access: Access to the Reading Rooms is free to all persons holding a valid Reader's Ticket. These are issued on production of some documentary proof of identity. In the case of non-UK citizens, this must be a passport or national identity card.

See: Jones pp. 168–207, MWP pp. 158–184, Pearson p. 53.

ST. ANDREWS

St. Andrews University Library   ■

Address:	St. Andrews University Library,
	North Street,
	St. Andrews KY16 9TR,
	Scotland.
Tel:	01334 462281
Fax:	01334 462282

The present University Library was refounded by James VI and dates from 1611–1612. Notable early printed books acquired by the Library in the Middle Eastern field include: The Gospels in Arabic (Rome 1591), the *Liber Psalmorum* in Arabic and Latin (Rome 1614), and Euclid in Arabic (Rome 1594). Among the modern books, the worldwide coverage of Islam concentrates mainly on the Middle East but there is also some material on North and West Africa and Moorish Spain. The growth over the past decade of Departments of International Relations and Social Anthropology has significantly strengthened the Library's holdings in this field.

Approximate numbers of books (including periodical volumes) and manuscripts: Islam 600; Arabic language and literature 6000; Middle East history 6000; Middle Eastern manuscripts c.80.

Access: Access to the Main Library is available to staff and students of the University and to others on application to the Librarian.

See: Auch. pp. 78–80, MWP p. 374, Pearson pp. 61, 118, 145, 320, Roman p. 49, Roper 3 pp. 525–526.

SHEFFIELD

■ ## Sheffield University Library

Address:	Sheffield University Library,
	Western Bank,
	Sheffield S10 2TN
Tel:	0114 282 4333
Fax:	0114 273 9826
Telex:	54348 ULSHEF G

There is no specialist collection of Middle Eastern material. Much of the material purchased is used by the Department of Biblical Studies. The major scholarly journals are subscribed to by the Library. The Middle Eastern book stock is mainly monograph material with some sets of published papers e.g. Weizmann. Apart from the books enumerated below, there are small numbers of books in other areas of the Library (e.g. geography, economics etc.) such as one would expect to find in a general academic library.

Approximate numbers of books: Biblical Studies and Judaism c.600 vols.; Middle East politics and contemporary history c.400 vols.

Access: Visitors are allowed to read in the Library but cannot borrow.

SOUTHAMPTON

Parkes Library, University of Southampton ■

Address:	The Parkes Library, University of Southampton, Highfield, Southampton SO9 5NH.
Tel:	01703 593335/593724 (Special Collections Division)
Fax:	01703 593007
e-mail:	library@uk.ac.soton
JANET:	See above

The Parkes Library is a special collection of 14,000 books, 360 sets of periodicals and 2500 pamphlets on the relationship between the Jewish and non-Jewish worlds, presented to the University of Southampton by the Rev. Dr. James Parkes in 1964. The Parkes Library covers the history of Jewish communities throughout the world, the history of Palestine and development of Zionism, Arab–Jewish relations, Christian–Jewish relations and anti-Semitism. A range of reprographic facilities is available.

Access (including catalogue access): A subject index, together with classified and author card catalogues, are available in the Reading Room; all periodicals and items acquired or recatalogued since 1981 are on OPAC. (OPAC is available via JANET: NRS address: 0000 5030 0017, NRS name soton.lib) For access to the Parkes Library, application should be made to the Librarian i/c Special Collections.

See: Jones p. 225, MWP p. 339.

Southampton University Library ■

See under: SOUTHAMPTON: Parkes Library, University of Southampton.

SOUTHPORT

■ Atkinson Library

Address: The Atkinson Library,
              Lord Street,
              Southport,
              Merseyside PR8 1DJ
Tel: 0151 934 2118/9

The Library has no separate Middle Eastern collections. However, under the North West Regional Libraries Subject Specialisation Scheme, Southport Public Libraries (now part of the Sefton Libraries and Arts Services) were allocated the following subjects: Iran/Persia, Turkey etc. (but not Arabia); Other languages (i.e. Dewey nos. 490–499); and Criticism of other languages (i.e. Dewey nos. 890–899). During the period c.1953/4–1979 all works in the BNB on these subjects (to a price ceiling of about £10) were bought for the Southport collections and are now integrated into the Sefton Libraries collections either in store or in stock. The Southport branch holds the largest number of items. (NB This type of material is no longer bought under this scheme.)

Access: The Library is open to all members of the public.

STIRLING

Stirling University Library ∎

Address:	Stirling University Library,
	Stirling FK9 4LA,
	Scotland
Tel:	01786 467235 (Information Desk)
Fax:	01786 466866
e-mail:	library@uk.ac.stirling
Internet:	lib.stir.ac.uk

The Library was founded in 1966 and houses a general academic collection of nearly 500,000 volumes. The Religious Studies section contains c.500 vols. on Islamic religion and life, while a further c.1500 vols. on various aspects of Islam and the Middle East are distributed as appropriate throughout the rest of the Library. Virtually all of this material is in English.

Access: The University operates an academic year of two semesters. Intending visitors are advised to confirm opening times and dates in advance, and to consult the Information Desk for all matters relating to reading and borrowing.

TODMORDEN

■ **Todmorden Branch Library**

Address:	Todmorden Branch Library,
	The Strand,
	Todmorden,
	Lancs. OL14 7LB
Tel:	01706 815600
Fax:	01706 819025

This is a branch library under the aegis of the Metropolitan Borough of Calderdale. With the beginning of local government reorganisation in 1973, the Library ceased to belong to the North West Area and, consequently, to the Area's subject specialisation scheme. As part of the latter, the Library collected books on Africa (including Egypt and the Sudan) in the fields of travel and history. The Library still retains some of this collection but it has not been added to since 1972. There is also a collection of adult and junior books written in Urdu and a small collection of adult and junior books on Islam retained as part of the normal stock.

Access: The Library is open to the general public.

YORK

J.B. Morrell Library, University of York ■

Address:	J.B. Morrell Library,
	University of York,
	Heslington,
	York YO1 5DD
Tel:	01904 433863
Fax:	01904 433866

The Library has a moderate collection of books on Islam and the Middle East originally ordered to support courses in history and politics. This material is almost entirely in Western languages.

Approximate numbers of books: There are significant under-graduate collections on: Islamic religion c.500 books; on Middle Eastern politics c.500; and on Middle Eastern history c.1000.

Access: Potential users should consult the issue desk in the first instance.

York University Library ■

See under: YORK: J.B. Morrell Library, University of York

Appendix One

Public Record Office of Northern Ireland

Middle East Records

D. 3574

Records of the Royal Irish Fusiliers and of the militia regiments which were its precursors, 1808–1957.

D.3574/C/   : Notes on the History of the Royal Irish Fusiliers
D.3574/E/4/   : Sudan
D.3574/E/6/   : World War I

DEPOSITED BY THE TRUSTEES OF THE REGIMENTAL MUSEUM OF THE ROYAL IRISH FUSILIERS

Notes on the History of the R.I.F.

D.3574/C/	*Date*	*Description*
1	1 Apr. 1920–31 Mar. 1921	Typescript notes on the history of the 1st Batt. R.I.F. in Iraq and N.W. Persia.
2	1931–39	File entitled historical records of the 2nd Batt. R.I.F. containing typescript notes, letters, etc.
3	1 Apr. 1937–31 Mar. 1938	Typescript notes comprising a daily record, reports on re-formation, and sports records of the 1st Batt. R.I.F.

Sudan

D.3574/E/4/	Date	Description
1	July–Sep. 1898	Large diary of the Sudan expedition kept by Brevet-Major D.W. Churcher, with manuscript descriptions, photographs, cartoons, and newspaper cuttings.
2	1898–1900	8 letters from Capt. Malcolm Wilson, 1st Batt., R.I.F. in Omdurman, Sudan and Nigeria, to his brother Robin, together with sketch maps of the areas; telegram and letter announcing Malcolm Wilson's death.

World War I

D.3574/E/6/	Date	Description
15	18 May 1915; 3 June 1915; 16 June 1915; 21 Aug. 1919	Letters from J.T. Penrose to Col. Burrowes relating to the death and diary of E.J.M. Penrose; letter from Col. C.R. Burn to Burrowes (?) reporting that Penrose is missing.
16	15 Dec. 1916	Letter from Mary Bull, Canterbury, Kent, the mother of Brig. Gen. George Bull, DSO to General Burrowes, relating to the death of her son, with newspaper obituary notice attached.
17A,B,C	1917–18	Diaries of A.J. Smith, on active service with 'B' Coy, (Princess Victoria's) 2nd Batt. Royal Irish Fusiliers, on active service in Palestine and Egypt, 1917–19. Illustrated with photographs.
18	10 June	Letter from J.S. [?] Burrowes, Buckingham, to her son, General Burrowes, giving news of family and friends. He refers to the wounding of Major Shuter and hopes that the regiment's officers will meet with their due reward, etc.
19	1918	3 documents. Papers relating to Major John George Brew, 9th Batt. R.I.F. including a certificate marking his mention in despatches, a commemorative scroll, and a photograph of his gravestone.
20	29 Sep. 1920; 15 Nov. 1920; 22 June 1922; 30 June 1922	4 letters to General Burrowes, dealing mainly with Penrose's diary, between his father John T. Penrose and General Burrowes.
21	25 Sep. 1920; 2 Oct. 1920; 2 Nov. 1920	3 letters from James Millar, Belfast, to General Burrowes, The White House, Buckingham, relating to the location of his son's grave and assisting in the compilation of a history of the 1st Batt. R.I.F.
22	28 Oct. 1923	Letter from Westropp, editor of *The Faugh A Ballagh* to General Burrowes, relating to the publication of Penrose's diary in the journal.

D.1581

c.600 documents; 28 volumes; 8 files; 6 photographs; wills, title deeds etc. relating to the Pollock family, Ballymoney, Co. Antrim; and correspondence, diaries and papers of Mr. and Mrs. J.H.H. Pollock, latterly residing at 'Drumcairne', Stewartstown, Co. Tyrone; 1781–1961.

J.H.H. Pollock served as Lieutenant, Captain and Major in the 6th Royal Irish Rifles, during World War I; in OETA Palestine 1919–1920 when he was demobilised; as Administrative Officer, Nigeria, 1923; Assistant Secretary to the Nigerian Secretariat in Lagos, 1927; District Commissioner in Haifa, 1939; and in Jerusalem, 1944–1948; and Chief Advisor to GOC British Troops in Palestine, 1948.

D.1581/2/:   Personal Correspondence of Mr. and Mrs. J.H.H. Pollock
D.1581/3/:   Diaries and Notebooks of Mr. and Mrs. J.H.H. Pollock
D.1581/4/:   Reports, Booklets, Correspondence etc. relating to Pollock's Work in Palestine and Nigeria
D.1581/5/:   Miscellaneous

DEPOSITED BY JAMES H.H. POLLOCK ESQ.

Personal Correspondence of Mr. and Mrs. J.H.H. Pollock

D.1581/2/	Date	Description
1	1914–1915	c.70 letters, mainly from J.H.H. Pollock, 6th Royal Irish Rifles, to his parents Mr. and Mrs. W. Charles Pollock, 'Ishlan', Ballymoney, Co. Antrim mainly from Trinity College, Dublin training camp and New Park Camp, Basingstoke, Hampshire.
2	1916–1917	c.35 letters mainly from Lieut. J.H.H. Pollock on active service in Salonika, Malta and Alexandria, to his parents.
3	1918	c.50 letters mainly from J.H.H. Pollock on active service in the Holy Land and Egypt?, to his parents.
4	1919–1920	c.15 letters from Mrs. Margaret Pollock, wife of J.H.H. Pollock on field service in Jerusalem, to her parents-in-law, Mr. and Mrs. W. Charles Pollock, Ballymoney, Co. Antrim.
5	1919–1921	c.25 letters mainly from J.H.H. Pollock on field service in Jerusalem and Ramallah, Palestine, to his parents.
6	1924–1928	c.15 letters from J.H.H. Pollock, Administrative Officer in Nigeria, 1923–1927, and subsequently Assistant Secretary to the Nigeria Secretariat in Lagos, to his parents.
7	1925–1927	6 letters from Mrs Margaret Pollock from various places in West Africa, to her parents-in-law, Mr. and Mrs. W. Charles Pollock, Ballymoney, Co. Antrim, 1925–1926, and letter of thanks to Mrs. Margaret Pollock from the Lieutenant-Governor, Southern Provinces, Lagos, Nigeria, 1927.
8	2 Sep. 1939	Letter from J.H.H. Pollock in Haifa, to his father.
9	1932; 1947–1948	c.150 letters from J.H.H. Pollock to his wife, from Haifa, Jerusalem, London, etc.
10	1946–1955	c.10 miscellaneous letters to Mr. and Mrs. J.H.H. Pollock, 'Drumcairne', Stewartstown, Co. Tyrone, two of them from [Lord?] Charlemont.

Diaries and Notebooks of Mr. and Mrs. J.H.H. Pollock

D.1581/3/	Date	Description
1	Aug. 1915	Field message book of J.H.H. Pollock, Royal Irish Rifles. (Very few entries.)
2	Aug.–Oct. 1924	Diary of J.H.H. Pollock, Administrative Officer in Nigeria.
3	Feb. 1926–? 1927	Notebook of Mrs. Pollock with accounts of events of some days in Feb. and April 1926 and Feb.–Apr., 1927 in Cameroon, West Africa.
4	1930	Diary of J.H.H. Pollock, who was working in Palestine.
5	1931	Diary of J.H.H. Pollock, who was working in Palestine.
6	1932	Diary of J.H.H. Pollock, who was working in Palestine.
7	Jan.–Feb. 1932	Mrs. Margaret Pollock's diary.
8	1933	Diary of J.H.H. Pollock who was working in Palestine.
9	1934	Diary of J.H.H. Pollock who was working in Palestine.
10A–D	Apr.–Oct. 1936	3 small volumes labelled 'Palestine Government' and another volume in which J.H.H. Pollock recorded events in detail.
11	c.1936	Notebook of J.H.H. Pollock containing very rough notes.
12	1937–1945	Notebook of J.H.H. Pollock containing rough notes.
13	Jan.–Feb. 1938	Diary of J.H.H. Pollock who was working in Palestine.
14	Jan.–Dec. 1938	Diary, kept by ? re. some events in Palestine and some engagements of J.H.H. Pollock, ADC.
15	1938	Diary of J.H.H. Pollock with very brief entries.
16	1940–1942	ARP diary of ?.

Diaries and Notebooks of Mr. and Mrs. J.H.H. Pollock

D.1581/3/	Date	Description
17	Jan.–May 1944	Diary of J.H.H. Pollock, District Commissioner in Palestine.
18	Jan.–Feb. 1945	Diary of J.H.H. Pollock, District Commissioner in Palestine.
19	1945	Engagement diary of Mrs. Margaret Pollock?
20	1948	Diary of J.H.H. Pollock, who became Chief Adviser to GOC British Troops in Palestine, 1948.

Reports, Booklets, Correspondence, etc. relating to Pollock's work in Palestine and Nigeria

D.1581/4/	Date	Description
1	1919	File of petitions and cases of poor Jews whom Zionists failed to support in their quest for work.
2	1920–1923	File containing reports re relief situation in Jerusalem, Greek Orthodox housing, correspondence, etc.
3	1921; 1931–1950	c.50 documents relating to the Pollocks' official position in Palestine: invitations, letters re honorary membership of various organisations, programmes of events and organisations of which J.H.H. Pollock was patron, etc.
4	1922	File of typed material re the Ceremony of the Holy Fire celebrated in the Church of the Holy Sepulchre, Jerusalem. (Includes a section re precautionary measures to be taken.)
5	c.1925–1951	File containing reports, etc. relating mainly to Palestine, and also to Nigeria.
6	1926–1960	Bulky file containing reports, extracts and instructions re to J.H.H. Pollock's work chiefly in Palestine, and also in Nigeria.
7A–D	1930–1947	4 official printed booklets re the administration and government of Palestine.
8	1931–1948	c.30 newspaper extracts concerning events in Palestine and J.H.H. Pollock personally.
9	c.1935–1951	File of 'semi official' notes and papers of J.H.H. Pollock.
10	c.1938–1961	File containing correspondence addressed to J.H.H. Pollock, booklets etc. relating to Palestine.
11	1940–1946	File of reports, correspondence addressed to Mrs. Margaret Pollock, wife of J.H.H. Pollock, etc. relating to the Red Cross in Palestine and Transjordan. (Mrs. Pollock was Vice-President of the Red Cross in Haifa, 1940–1942 and subsequently for the Jerusalem district.)

Reports, Booklets, Correspondence, etc. relating to Pollock's work in Palestine and Nigeria

D.1581/4/	Date	Description
12	1940–1947; 1956	c.65 letters mainly to Mrs. Margaret Pollock in Palestine, where her husband was District Commissioner, from various people, thanking her for kindness, etc. she had shown them in the course of her husband's duties.

Miscellaneous

D.1581/5	Date	Description
1	1914–1920	Army service record book of J.H.H. Pollock.
2	c.1920–1921	Autograph book (very few entries) belonging to the Pollocks.
3	c.1925	6 small black and white photographs, mainly of tribal chiefs in West Africa.
4	1940–1947	Extract from visitors' book of the Pollocks (in loose leaf format).
5	1943–1956	Autograph book of J.H.H. Pollock.
6	1946	Leather wallet containing identity card and other official pass cards of J.H.H. Pollock, District Commissioner, Jerusalem district.

D.3480/52

Papers of General F.R. Chesney

Papers of General F.R. Chesney

D.3480/52	Date	Description
1	1829–1831	An unpublished autobiographical draft narrative of Chesney's travels to Turkey, Greece, Egypt, Lebanon and Syria, and an account of his initial exploration of the Euphrates Valley.
2	1830–1831	Bound manuscript of Chesney's formal report on his exploration of the Euphrates Valley and Survey of the Isthmus of Suez, including a map and some detailed drawings of a steamer, written out neatly in sections in the hands of several amanuenses with additions in Chesney's hand. Although apparently unpublished, the report was incorporated into a 2 volume tome published in 1858: the manuscript is probably important as documenting the information available to British officialdom and acted on by them over 25 years.
3	1834–1835	Three letters from the Admiralty regarding the supply of provisions by Royal Navy agents at Malta to the Euphrates Expedition under the leadership of Colonel Chesney.
4	1836–1837	Collection of newspaper cuttings relating to the Euphrates Valley expedition under the leadership of Colonel Chesney. Five of Chesney's letterbooks, 1823–1871, containing copies or drafts of c.400 letters sent and received, partly in Chesney's own hand and partly in the hands of amanuenses. The letters include much relating to the Euphrates expeditions, both before and afterwards, including his plans, estimates of cost notes on the instruments used and the steamships assembled in segments on the expedition, possible alternative routes to India in view of the movements of the Pasha of Egypt, and Chesney's many attempts to recover from the Treasury his considerable expenses. Some of the letters relate to the publication of his books, to the woodcuts and lithographs that appeared in them and to copies presented to Queen Victoria and Napoleon III.

Papers of General F.R. Chesney

D.3480/52	Date	Description
		Other letters relate to his career in China, military matters including the events leading to the outbreak of the Crimean War, the reorganisation of the Royal Artillery, his ideas on the future of telegraphic communication, a proposed award to him for saving the crew of a shipwreck in 1814; and personal matters, including the breaking off of his engagement to Miss Fraser and the illness of his wife, Louisa.
5	1823–1829	Letterbook of F.R. Chesney.
6	1838–1842	Letterbook of F.R. Chesney.
7	1846–1847	Letterbook of F.R. Chesney.
8	1850–1856	Letterbook of F.R. Chesney.
9	1857–1871	Letterbook of F.R. Chesney.
10	1861	Booklet containing biographical details of General F.R. Chesney and genealogical notes on his family published by a French company as part of a series about famous European families and individuals.
11	c.1870	Notes prepared by Edward Stanford about a treatise written by an Austrian army officer, 1858, about the possibility of a railway through the Euphrates Valley.
12	1871–1872; 1885	Album of newspaper cuttings, most of which relate to the death of General Chesney on 30 January 1872. The obituary notices provide useful biographical information about his life and career.
13	1850	*Expedition to the Euphrates and Tigris by Col. Chesney*, Vols. I and II, and boxed set of maps, [1835–1837] (published London, 1850).

Appendix Two

Modern Records Centre, University of Warwick

Middle East Records

— *Federation of British Industries*

— *Papers of the Publisher and Humanitarian, Sir Victor Gollancz*

— *The Case of Adolf Eichmann*

— *Standard Motor Company*

— *TUC*

— *Papers of Richard Crossman (1907–1974)*

Federation of British Industries

Files of Sir Norman Kipping, Director General of the Federation of British Industries, including re Middle East topics and visits, *c.* 1948–62. (MSS.200/F/3/D3)

Overseas Department of the FBI: a few files re Middle East, especially trade with, post-1945. (MSS.200/F/3/O)

Papers of the Publisher and Humanitarian, Sir Victor Gollancz (MSS.157)

Anglo-Israel Association: 2 files re VG's involvement, 1949–62, 1961–7.

Arab Development Society: file re political problems created by VG's appeal on behalf of the Society, published as a news item in *The Times*, 1961.

Jewish Affairs (mainly in UK): a group of files (mainly post-1945) including correspondence with individuals and organisations on such topics as invitations to speak, charitable activity, Jewish–Arab relations, Friends of the Hebrew University of Jerusalem, ritual slaughter.

Jewish Society for Human Service: 10 files (1948–67) re VG's involvement in the Society, which he called together as a small group in 1948. Main topics: fund-raising, aid to Arab refugees.

The Case of Adolf Eichmann (pub. 1961): 3 files (1961–2), the largest dealing with reaction to the pamphlet and including an exchange with Berl Locker.

Standard Motor Company

File re Leyland-Triumph (Israel) Ltd. and acquisition of interest in Autocars Co. Ltd., 1964–5/6. (3 subsequent files, 1966–7, 1969–71, subject to 30-year rule.) (MSS.226/ST/3/O/IS/1–4)

Data re sales to Iraq Petroleum Co., 1952 (MSS.226/ST/3/A/PRO/3).

TUC

Files re Middle East (MSS.292/956), 1928–60, including 8 re Palestine/Israel.

Files re Egypt, 1926–60 (MSS.292/962/1–8).

MSS.154   Papers of Richard Crossman (1907–1974)

MSS.154/3/AU/1/1–512

Includes RHSC's notes of a conversation at the Foreign Office with Lord Henderson and Harold Beeley re British recognition of Israel, Sep 1948 (/214–19); correspondence with Emir Abdul Majid Haidar re Jordan,

Mar 1951 (/293–8); notes by RHSC on Suez and Sudan, Jan 1953 (/321–6); Anwar Sadat re the Sudan, Feb 1953 (/327); G.A. Nasser re RHSC's speeches on Anglo-Egyptian relations, Apr 1953 (/328–9).

MSS.154/3/JE/1–559

Correspondence re Jewish and Israeli affairs, 1947–1974.

Mainly 1968 onwards; arranged in chronological order. Includes: 'Report to the General Assembly by the United Nations Special Committee on Palestine', 1947 (/4–100); correspondence re Shechita (/Jewish method of slaughtering animals), 1968 (/110–25); mainly invitations to social events or to speak or write, e.g. to the Labour Friends of Israel. Also includes ltr., Meyer W. Weisgal-RHSC re the proposed biography of Weizmann, enclosing a copy of a letter from Isaiah Berlin which comments on RHSC's appointment as editor of *The New Statesman*, 1970 (/128a–b).

MSS.154/3/LIT/5/1–184

File re reviews for *Commentary*, 1948–63.

Some correspondence, TS and pr. reviews, especially reviews of books re Palestine and Anglo-Jewish relations.

MSS.154/3/LIT/13–16

Files re RHSC's projected biography of Chaim Weizmann, 1962, 1970–4.

RHSC's ill-health forced him to abandon the project in Jan 1974 and it was taken up by Walter C. Laqueur. Laqueur also failed to finish; the biography was finally published in 1985: Jehuda Reinharz, *Chaim Weizmann. The making of a Zionist leader* (OUP, 1985).

MSS.154/3/LIT/13/1–170

File re RHSC's contribution to memorial volume to Weizmann: ed. M.W. Weisgal and J. Carmichael, *Chaim Weizmann, a biography by several hands* (London, 1962).

Includes RHSC's draft chapter, (/1–29, 68–110), his commemorative address at Columbia University, 4 Dec 1962 (/30–67), some transcriptions and copies of related Weizmann letters (/113) and reflections or interviews with Weizmann's contemporaries and family (/117–45, 150–70).

MSS.154/3/LIT/14/1–93

Correspondence re RHSC's biography of Weizmann, 1970–1.

Includes correspondence with Sir George Weidenfeld (publisher), RHSC's solicitor, and Meyer Weisgal, chairman of Yad Chaim Weizmann.

MSS.154/3/LIT/15/1–219

Correspondence as above, 1972.

Includes correspondence with Weizmann contemporaries, and research associates.

MSS.154/3/LIT/16/1–341

Correspondence as above, 1973–4.

Includes correspondence re RHSC's withdrawal from the project because of his ill-health.

MSS.154/3/LIT/22/1–20

Correspondence re article on Israel, included in *The Jew*, published by Douglas Villiers Publishing Ltd, 1972–3.

MSS.154/3/LP/2/1–185

Labour Party correspondence, circulars and press releases, 1951, 1960–73.

Includes note by RHSC on Middle East, 1955 (/8–12); note by RHSC of a conversation with Col. Nasser, 1955 (/13–18).

MSS.154/3/POL/1–582

Miscellaneous political correspondence and papers, 1956–1973. Many annotated 'diary' or 'keep'; arranged in chronological order.

Includes RHSC's notes on the United Nations and the Middle Eastern crisis, Feb 1957 (/61–3); ltr., Eliahu Elath (Israeli ambassador)–RHSC, re Arab unity, Jul 1958 (/147); ltr., RHSC-E. Elath, re Arab unification, Aug 1958 (/161); ltr., RHSC–Golda Meir, Israeli Foreign Minister, re same, Aug 1958 (/162–4); correspondence betw. RHSC & Dolek Horowitz, Governor, Bank of Israel, re Eichmann trial, Apr 1961 (/339–42).

MSS.154/3/WI/1–59

Correspondence and papers re the Weizmann Institute, 1964, 1973–4.

RHSC was elected a member of the Board of Governors of the Weizmann Institute of Science in 1964. Mainly correspondence, agenda and minutes re meetings of the governors, 1964, 1973–4. Also includes correspondence with Rinna Samuel re her biography of Golda Meir [Samuel was working at the Weizmann Institute], 1973–4 (/19–22, 44–6, 50–2).

MSS.154/3/ZB/786–866

Correspondence between Crossman and his second wife, Zita Baker, 1939–47 letters. *Not open for research.*

Letters include several written during his work for the Anglo-American Committee of Enquiry regarding the problems of European Jewry and Palestine (the Palestine Commission), Dec 1945–April 1946 (/803–15); and RHSC's letter re an attack on the Labour government's foreign policy, 14 Nov 1946 (/876). [More of RHSC's Palestine Commission papers, including diary entries enclosed with some of these letters, are deposited in Oxford in the Middle East Centre Library, St. Antony's College (*qv*), ref. DS 126.4. *See* RHSC, *Palestine Mission. A personal record* (/1947).]

MSS.154/4/BR/6–10

'International Commentary', BBC Hebrew Service, Jul 1953–Sep 1964. A fortnightly series.

MSS.154/4/BR/10/1–229

Broadcasts, Jan 1963–Sep 1964.
Includes correspondence with James Monahan re U.N. refugee camps in Palestine, Feb 1964 (/110–12).

Appendix Three

Scottish Record Office

Middle East Records

[NB The starred collections are accessible to the Scottish Record Office online catalogue search system, CLIO]

1 Ref: GD1/633: *Records deposited by J.H. Loch.* Among these are 2 diaries of Francis Erskine Loch, compiled from notes he made as a naval commander in the Persian Gulf, 1818–1821.

2 GD40/17: *Papers of Philip Kerr, 11th Marquess of Lothian 1882–1940:* Files as Private Secretary to Lloyd George.

GD40/17/37–41	Middle East 1917–20 (Turkey, Syria, Palestine, Iraq, Armenia, Middle East delegates at Paris peace conference, Zionism).
GD40/17/42:	Zionism, 1917.

Other Papers:

GD40/17/131–132:	Palestine – papers and pamphlets, 1930.
GD40/17/205:	Palestine – letters re Dr. Chaim Weizmann, 1917–1940.

General Correspondence:

GD/40/17/206–220:	1918–21, inc. letters on Palestine, Mesopotamia, Syria, Middle East in general.
GD40/17/347:	1937, Palestine.
GD40/17/358:	1937–8, letter from Edward Thompson regarding visit to Egypt and Syria.

Additional Papers:

GD40/17/1339–1351:	Correspondence and papers regarding the Middle East 1919–21: Syrian mandate, Mesopotamia.

3 GD45: *Dalhousie Muniments.* Include papers of the 10th Earl and 1st Marquess of Dalhousie as Governor General of India (Section 6).

This extensive part of the collections contains many items of relevance to Islam in India. The main item of Middle East relevance is:

GD45/7/507–519:	Papers concerning relations with Persia, Russia and Afghanistan 1836–1857.

4 GD51 *Melville Castle Muniments* – papers of 1st Viscount Melville, President of the India Board, Secretary for War, First Lord of the Admiralty:

GD51/1/768–805:	Letters regarding Bonaparte's expedition to Egypt, Egyptian campaign, 1798–1801.

GD51/1/550:   Letter from the Earl of Elgin to Pitt regarding Turkey, Russo-Turkish relations, Sir Sydney Smith, 1800.

GD51/1/590:   Letter from Captain Campbell regarding establishment of a mission to the Persian Court, 1828.

5* GD136 *Sinclair of Freswick Muniments:*

GD136/1187:   Notes on expenses of a visit to Egypt (19th Century).

GD136/1214:   General orders approving the conduct of the army in Egypt, 16 May 1801.

6* GD155: *Maxton – Graham of Cultoquhey Muniments.*

GD155/874:   Letter from Anthony Maxtone of Cuttoquhey describing the journey of the Indian Army to Egypt via the Red Sea, 1800.

GD155/1253:   Letter describing the state of French forces in Egypt, 9 September 1798.

GD155/1259:   List of French military commanders in the different provinces of Egypt.

7* GD164: *Rosslyn Muniments.*

GD164/1703:   Letter from Frederick Stewart at Calcutta regarding relations with the Vizier, Shujah al Dewlah, 1772–5.

8* GD172: *Henderson of Fordell Muniments.*

GD172/141:   Letter from R Keppel Craven, Naples: attack by mob on Arab sailors, 1842–51.

9   GD261: *Papers of Sir Charles Augustus Murray*, diplomatist employed in various posts including Egypt and Persia.

GD261/6:   Notebook containing Murray's journal of his voyage from Suez to Muscat, the Gulf, Baghdad and Babylon, 1855.

GD261/8:   Notes of Murray's journey from Teheran to Tiflis, 1859.

GD261/10:   Murray's 'Memorandum of some of the Principal Events accompanying and following my Mission to Persia', 1854–5.

GD261/11:   Copies of Murray's official correspondence as Ambassador to Persia, 1857.

GD261/12:	MS. volume of phrases and idioms in Arabic, Turkish and Persian.
GD261/13:	Murray's commonplace book.
GD261/15:	MS. Sentences and Proverbs from Goulistan.
GD261/16:	Small volume containing illuminated oriental MS ('Bāznāmeh, a treatise on falconry written expressly for me by Prince Timour Marca at Baghdad ... with some notes thereon by Dr. Rieu of the British Museum').
GD261/17:	Typescript copies of letters from Hugh Thurburn to Murray on Egyptian affairs, 1863–1876.
GD261/20:	Volume containing précis of Col. Taylor's despatches from Herat, 1858 and the 'secret series of letters from Teheran', 1857.
GD261/21:	Official instructions to Murray on his appointment as Ambassador to Persia, 1854.
GD261/22:	Notebook containing Murray's journal of a journey from Basra to Baghdad, 1857.
GD261/28:	Letters from Murray in Persia to his brother Admiral the Hon. Henry Murray, 1825–1857.
GD261/31:	Murray's 'letter in Persian to the Shah of Persia', 1859 (copy).
GD261/26:	'Eastern' and Other Notes by Hon Sir C.A. Murray.
GD261/38:	Autograph letters from eminent personages inc Lord Stratford de Redcliffe on Egyptian affairs, Sir Henry Baliver on Persian affairs.
GD261/39, 42, 48, 55, 56 57, 60:	Bundles of miscellaneous letters including items relating to Egypt and Persia.

10 GD371:   *Papers of Sir John McNeill.* These include correspondence and papers from his time as envoy and plenipotentiary to the Shah of Persia 1835–45, and earlier when attached to the legation in Persia (I enclose a copy of the Contents page from this collection's catalogue).

11 GD391:   *Stewart-Peter papers.* Includes correspondence and photographs from Robert H. Stewart-Peter's service with the navy in the Mediterranean (1917–23) and the RAF in Iraq (1924–7).

12 GD433/2:   *Muniments of A.J. Balfour, 1st Earl Balfour.* Includes correspondence and papers relating to Palestine and Zionism 1916–1930. Much of the collection is normally consulted on microfilm. These papers were formerly at the family residence at Whittinghame, and are supplementary to the main set of Balfour's papers in the British Library (*qv*).

13 RH4/84/1–4:   Diaries and autobiography of General Sir Spencer Ewart. (Microfilm). Includes accounts of his service in Egypt 1882–1895. (Original *penes* Monro of Williamwood.)

Bibliography

This bibliography is restricted mainly to those catalogues, directories and works cited in this Directory.

Abbot, T.K. *Catalogue of the Manuscripts in the Library of Trinity College, Dublin*, (Dublin: Hodges, Figgis & Co./London: Longmans, Green & Co., 1900).

Allan, Nigel 'Catalogue of Hebrew Manuscripts in the Wellcome Institute, London', *JSS*, Vol. 27 (1982), pp. 193–220.

Allan, Nigel 'Catalogue of Hebrew Printed Books (1491–1900) in the Wellcome Institute, London', *JSS*, Vol. 39 (1994), pp. 183–206.

Allan, Nigel 'The Oriental Collections in the Wellcome Institute for the History of Medicine, London', *JRAS*, No. 1 (1981), pp. 10–25.

Allan, Nigel 'Syriac Fragments in the Wellcome Institute Library', *JRAS*, No. 1 (1987), pp. 43–47.

Arberry, A.J. *The Chester Beatty Library: A Handlist of the Arabic Manuscripts*, (Vols. 1–2: Dublin: Emery Walker (Ireland) Ltd., 1955–1956; Vols. 3–8: Dublin: Hodges, Figgis & Co., 1958–1966). [Vol. 8 (indexes) was compiled by Ursula Lyons.]

Arberry, A.J. *The Koran Illuminated: A Handlist of the Korans in the Chester Beatty Library*, (Dublin: Hodges Figgis, 1967).

Arberry, A.J. *et al.* *The Chester Beatty Library: A Catalogue of the Persian Manuscripts and Miniatures*, 3 Vols., (Dublin: Hodges Figgis, 1959–1962):
  Vol. 1: By A.J. Arberry, M. Minovi & E. Blochet, ed. by J.V.S. Wilkinson (1959).
  Vol. 2: By M. Minovi, B.W. Robinson, J.V.S. Wilkinson & E. Blochet, ed. by A.J. Arberry (1960).
  Vol. 3: By A.J. Arberry, B.W. Robinson, J.V.S. Wilkinson, & E. Blochet, ed. by A.J. Arberry (1962).

Arberry, A.J.: *See also under*: Storey, C.A.

Auchterlonie, Paul (ed.), *Collections in British Libraries on Middle Eastern and Islamic Studies*, Occasional Papers Series No. 12, (Durham: University of Durham Centre for Middle Eastern and Islamic Studies, 1982).

Barringer, Terry A. 'The Rise, Fall and Rising Again of the Royal Commonwealth Society Library', *African Research and Documentation*, No. 64 (1994), pp. 1–10.

Beeston, A.F.L. 'The Oriental Manuscript Collections of the Bodleian Library', *Bodleian Library Record*, Vol. 5 (1954–1955), pp. 73–79.

Bond, Maurice F. *Guide to the Records of Parliament*, (London: HMSO, 1971).

Bosworth, C.E., Radwan, A.S. & Sa'id, S.A.M. *A Catalogue of Accessions to the Arabic Manuscripts in the John Rylands University Library of Manchester*, (Manchester: John Rylands University Library of Manchester, 1974).

Brady, David *Middle Eastern and Judaic Studies: A Guide to Research Resources*, (Manchester: John Rylands Library & Department of Middle Eastern Studies, 1995).

Browne, Edward G. *A Hand-list of the Muhammadan Manuscripts, Including All Those Written in the Arabic Character, Preserved in the Library of the University of Cambridge*, (Cambridge: Cambridge University Press, 1900).

Browne, Edward G. *A Supplementary Hand-list of the Muhammadan Manuscripts, Including All Those Written in the Arabic Character, Preserved in the Libraries of the University and Colleges of Cambridge*, (Cambridge: Cambridge University Press, 1922).

Codrington, O. 'Catalogue of the Arabic, Persian, Hindustani and Turkish MSS in the Library of the Royal Asiatic Society', *JRAS*, (1892), pp. 501–569.

Colonial Office *Catalogue of the Colonial Office Library*, (Boston: G.K. Hall, 1964, with supps. to 1977).

Cowley, A.E. *A Concise Catalogue of the Hebrew Printed Books in the Bodleian Library*, (Oxford: Clarendon Press, 1971).

Coxe, H.O. *Catalogus codicum mss qui in Collegiis aulisque Oxoniensibus hodie adservantur*, 2 Vols., (Oxford: Academic Press, 1852).

Daly, M.W. & Forbes, L.E. *The Sudan: Caught in Time*, (Reading: Garnet, 1994).

Davis, M.C. *A Catalogue of the Pre-1850 Books in the Cecil Roth Collection*, (Leeds: Brotherton Library, 1994).

Department of Education (Ireland) *Report of the Council of Trustees of the National Library of Ireland for 1977*, (Dublin: Stationery Office, nd).

Donkin, Winifred Cotterill *Catalogue of the Gertrude Bell Collection in the Library of King's College, Newcastle upon Tyne*, (Newcastle upon Tyne: King's College Library, 1960).

Edinburgh University Library *Oriental Manuscripts, a Continuation of the Descriptive Catalogue of 1925, by Hukk, Ethé & Robertson*, Handlist H9, (Edinburgh: Edinburgh University Library, 1994).

Ellis, A.G. *Catalogue of Arabic Books in the British Museum*:
Vols. 1–2: (London: British Museum, 1894–1901).
Vol. 3:   *Indexes* by A.S. Fulton, (London: British Museum, 1935).
          [Vols. 1–3 reprinted 1967]

Ethé, Herman *A Catalogue of Oriental Manuscripts, Persian, Arabic and Hindustani*, (Aberystwyth: National Library of Wales, 1916).

Forbes, Lesley 'The Sudan Archive of the University of Durham' in B.C.

Bloomfield (ed.), *Middle East Studies and Libraries: A Felicitation Volume for Professor J.D. Pearson*, (London: Mansell, 1980), pp. 49–57.

Foreign Office *Catalogue of Printed Books in the Library of the Foreign Office. 31st December 1885*, (London: Harrison & Sons, 1886).

Foreign Office *Catalogue of Printed Books in the Library of the Foreign Office*, (London: HM Stationery Office, 1926).

Foreign Office *Catalogue of the Foreign Office Library, 1926–1968*, (Boston: G.K. Hall, 1972).

Fulton, A.S. & Ellis, A.G. *Supplementary Catalogue of Arabic Printed Books in the British Museum*, (London: British Museum, 1926).

Fulton, A.S. & Lings, M. *Second Supplementary Catalogue of Arabic Printed Books in the British Museum, 1926–1957*, (London: British Museum, 1959).

Fulton, A.S.: *See also under*: Ellis, A.G.

Gacek, Adam *Catalogue of Arabic Manuscripts in the Library of the Institute of Ismaili Studies*:

Vol. 1: (London: Islamic Publications, 1984).

Vol. 2: (London: Islamic Publications, 1985).

Gacek, Adam *Catalogue of the Arabic Manuscripts in the Library of the School of Oriental and African Studies*, (London: SOAS, 1981).

Gordon, Lesley (comp.), *Gertrude Bell*, (Newcastle upon Tyne: University of Newcastle upon Tyne, 1994).

Gottschalk, H.L., Trimingham, J.S., Beeston, A.F.L. & Hopwood, Derek: *See under*: Mingana, A.

Green, V.H.H. *The Commonwealth of Lincoln College 1427–1977*, (Oxford: OUP, 1979).

Grimwood-Jones, Diana (ed.), *Middle East and Islam: A Bibliographical Introduction*, Bibliotheca Asiatica 15, rev. & enlarged edn., (Zug, Switzerland: Inter-Documentation Company, 1979).

Grimwood-Jones, Diana (ed.), *Sources for the History of the British in the Middle East 1800–1978. A Catalogue of the Private Papers Collection in the Middle East Centre, St. Antony's College, Oxford*, (London: Mansell, 1979).

Grimwood-Jones, Diana, Hopwood, Derek & Pearson, J.D. (eds.), *Arab Islamic Bibliography*, (Hassocks: Harvester Press/Atlantic Highlands, NJ: Humanities Press, 1977).

Haldane, Duncan *Islamic Bookbindings in the Victoria and Albert Museum*, (London: World of Islam Festival Trust in association with the Victoria and Albert Museum, 1983).

Hukk, M.A., Ethé, H. & Robertson, E. *A Descriptive Catalogue of the Arabic and Persian Manuscripts in the Edinburgh University Library*, (Printed for the University of Edinburgh by Stephen Austin & Sons Ltd., Hertford, 1925).

Iskandar, A.Z. *A Catalogue of Arabic Manuscripts on Medicine and Science in the Wellcome Historical Medical Library*, (London: Wellcome Historical Medical Library, 1967).

James, David *Qur'ans and Bindings from the Chester Beatty Library: A Facsimile Exhibition,* (London: World of Islam Festival Trust, 1980).

Jones, Philip *Britain and Palestine 1914–1918: Archival Sources for the History of the British Mandate,* (Oxford: Published for the British Academy by the OUP, 1979).

Kennedy, B.P. *Alfred Chester Beatty and Ireland 1950–1968: A Study in Cultural Politics,* (Dublin: Glendale Press, 1988).

Keshavarz, F. *Descriptive and Analytical Catalogue of Persian Manuscripts in the Library of the Wellcome Institute for the History of Medicine,* (London: Wellcome Institute, 1986).

Kirkpatrick, B.J. *A Catalogue of the Library of Sir Richard Burton KCMG Held by the Royal Anthropological Institute,* (London: RAI, 1978).

Kitchin, G.W. *Catalogus codicum mss qui in Bibliotheca Aedis Christi apud Oxonienses adservantur,* (Oxford: Clarendon Press, 1867).

Leach, Linda Y. *Mughal and Other Indian Paintings from the Chester Beatty Library,* 2 Vols., (London: Scorpion Cavendish, 1993).

Levy, R.: *See under:* Storey, C.A.

Lewin, Evans *The Subject Catalogue of the Royal Empire Society,* 4 Vols., (1930–1937, reprinted London: Dawsons, 1967).

Lieberman, Saul (ed.), *Alexander Marx: Jubilee Volume on the Occasion of His Seventieth Birthday* [English Section], (New York: Jewish Theological Seminary of America, 1950).

Lings, M. & Safadi, Y.H. *Third Supplementary Catalogue of Arabic Printed Books in the British Library 1958–1969,* 4 Vols., (London: British Library, 1977).

Loewe, H. *Catalogue of the Manuscripts in the Hebrew Character Collected and Bequeathed to Trinity College Library by the Late William Aldis Wright,* (Cambridge: Cambridge University Press, 1926).

Loth, O. *A Catalogue of the Arabic Manuscripts in the Library of the India Office,* (London: India Office, 1877).

Margoliouth, G. *Catalogue of the Hebrew and Samaritan Manuscripts in the British Museum,* 4 Vols., (London: British Museum, 1899–1933).

Matthews, Noel, Wainwright, M. Doreen & Pearson, J.D. (comps. & eds.), *A Guide to Manuscripts and Documents in the British Isles Relating to the Middle East and North Africa,* (Oxford: OUP, 1980).

McCarthy, Muriel *All Graduates and Gentlemen: Marsh's Library,* (Dublin: O'Brien Press, 1980).

Mingana, A. *Catalogue of the Arabic Manuscripts in the John Rylands Library, Manchester,* (Manchester: Manchester University Press, 1934).

Mingana, A. *Catalogue of the Mingana Collection of Manuscripts Now in the Possession of the Trustees of the Woodbrooke Settlement, Selly Park, Birmingham:*

Vol. 1 *Syriac and Garshuni Manuscripts,* (Cambridge: W. Heffer and Sons, 1933).

Vol. 2 *Christian Arabic Manuscripts and Additional Syriac Manuscripts*, (Cambridge: W. Heffer & Sons, 1936).

Vol. 3 *Additional Christian Arabic and Syriac Manuscripts*, (Cambridge: W. Heffer & Sons, 1939)

Vol. 4 *Islamic Arabic Manuscripts*, [by H.L. Gottschalk, J.S. Trimingham, A.F.L. Beeston & Derek Hopwood], (Birmingham: Selly Oak Colleges, 1963; rev. edn. edited by Derek Hopwood, Zug, Switzerland: IDC, 1985).

[The *Catalogue* has been made available *in microfiche* by the Inter-Documentation Company (IDC) AG, P.O.B. 11205, 2301 EE Leiden, The Netherlands.]

Minorsky, V. *The Chester Beatty Library: A Catalogue of the Turkish Manuscripts and Miniatures*, (Dublin: Hodges Figgis, 1958).

Moir, M. *A General Guide to the India Office Records*, (London: British Library, 1988).

Moorat, S.A.J. *Catalogue of Western Manuscripts on Medicine and Science in the Wellcome Historical Medical Library*, 3 Vols., (London: Wellcome Historical Medical Library, 1962–1973).

Morgan, Paul *Oxford Libraries Outside the Bodleian: A Guide*, (Oxford: Oxford Bibliographical Society & the Bodleian Library, 1973).

Munby, A.N.L. *Cambridge College Libraries*, 2nd edn., (Cambridge: W. Heffer & Sons, 1962).

National Library of Wales *Handlist of Manuscripts in the National Library of Wales*, (Aberystwyth: National Library of Wales, 1940).

Needham, Joseph *Science and Civilization in China*, (Cambridge: Cambridge University Press, 1954–continuing).

Nersessian, V. 'Cuc'ak hayaren jer'agrec 'London Velk'om Institute gradarani' [Catalogue of Armenian Manuscripts in the Wellcome Institute, London], *Banber Matenadarani*, No. 15 (1986), pp. 317–338.

Netton, Ian Richard *Middle East Materials in United Kingdom and Irish Libraries: A Directory*, A MELCOM Guide to Libraries and Other Institutions in Britain and Ireland with Islamic and Middle Eastern Books and Materials, (London: Library Association Publishing, 1983).

Neubauer, A. *A Catalogue of the Hebrew Manuscripts in the Bodleian Library and in the College Libraries of Oxford*, (Oxford: Clarendon Press, repr. 1994).

Oxford Centre for Postgraduate Hebrew Studies *The Kressel Collection*, (Oxford: Oxford Centre for Postgraduate Hebrew Studies 1981).

Palmer, E.H. *A Descriptive Catalogue of the Arabic, Persian and Turkish Manuscripts in the Library of Trinity College, Cambridge with an Appendix Containing a Catalogue of the Hebrew and Samaritan Mss in the Same Library*, (Cambridge: Deighton, Bell & Co., 1870).

Pearson, J.D. *Guide to Manuscripts and Documents in the British Isles Relating to Africa*, 2 Vols., (Oxford: OUP, 1993).

Pearson, J.D. *Oriental Manuscripts in Europe and North America: A Survey*, Bibliotheca Asiatica 7, (Zug, Switzerland: Inter-Documentation Company, 1971).

Quirke, S.G.J. & Tait, W.J. 'Egyptian Manuscripts in the Wellcome Collection', *Journal of Egyptian Archaeology*, No. 80 (1994), pp. 145–158.

Quraishi, S. 'Catalogue of Urdu, Panjabi and Kashmiri Manuscripts', *Journal of the Research Society of Pakistan, No. 23 (1987), pp. 53–70.*

Robson, James 'Catalogue of the Oriental Mss in the Library of the University of Glasgow' in C.J. Mullo Weir (ed.), *Presentation Volume to William Barron Stevenson*, Studia Semitica et Orientalia Vol. 2, (Glasgow: Glasgow University Oriental Society, 1945), pp. 116–137.

Roman, Stephan *The Development of Islamic Library Collections in Western Europe and North America*, Libraries and Librarianship in the Muslim World Series, (London & New York: Mansell, 1990).

Roper, Geoffrey (ed.) *World Survey of Islamic Manuscripts*, 4 Vols., (London: Al-Furqan Islamic Heritage Foundation, 1992–1994).

Rowland-Smith, D. (ed.), *Second Supplementary Catalogue of Hebrew Printed Books in the British Library, 1893–1960*, 2 Vols., (London: British Library, 1994).

Royal Asiatic Society *The Royal Asiatic Society: Its Activities and Objectives*, (London: Royal Asiatic Society, nd).

Royal Commonwealth Society *The Biography Catalogue*, (London: Royal Commonwealth Society, 1961).

Royal Commonwealth Society *The Subject Catalogue of the Royal Commonwealth Society*, 7 Vols., (Boston: G.K. Hall, 1971). [2 Supp. Vols. were issued in 1977.]

School of Oriental and African Studies *The SOAS, University of London, Library Catalogue* Author, Title and Subject Catalogues, (Boston: G.K. Hall):
   – Up to 1963:   28 Vols.
   – 1963–1968:   1st Supp. 18 Vols.
   – 1968–1973:   2nd Supp. 16 Vols.
   – 1973–1978:   3rd Supp. 19 Vols.
   – 1979–1989:   Supp. published on microfiche by IDC (The dates above refer to the acquisition periods covered by each Supp.)

Simmonds, Stuart & Digby, Simon (eds.) *The Royal Asiatic Society: Its History and Treasures*, (Published for the Royal Asiatic Society by Leiden/London: E.J. Brill, 1979).

Simpson, Donald H. (ed.), *The Manuscript Catalogue of the Library of the Royal Commonwealth Society*, (London: Mansell, 1975).

Sims-Williams, Ursula *Catalogue of the Arabic Manuscripts in the Library of the India Office, Volume 2: Index*, (London: British Library, 1991).

Sims-Williams, Ursula *Handlist of Islamic Manuscripts Acquired by the India Office Library, 1938–1985*, (London: India Office Library and Records, 1986).

Sims-Williams, Ursula (ed.) *Union Catalogue of Persian Serials and News-papers in British Libraries*, (London: Ithaca Press 1985).

Stokes, G.T. & Lawlor, H.J. (ed.), *Some Worthies of the Irish Church*, (London: Hodder & Stoughton, 1990).

Storey, C.A. *et al.* *Catalogue of the Arabic Manuscripts in the Library of the India Office Volume 2*:
 Fasc.1: *Qur'anic Literature* by C.A. Storey, (London: OUP for the India Office, 1930).
 Fasc.2: *Sufism and Ethics* by A.J. Arberry, (London: OUP for the India Office, 1936).
 Fasc.3: *Fiqh* by R. Levy, (London: India Office, 1937).
 Fasc.4: *Kalam* by R. Levy, (London: India Office, 1940).

Strelcyn, Stefan 'Catalogue of Ethiopian Manuscripts of the Wellcome Institute of the History of Medicine in London', *BSOAS*, Vol. XXXV (1972), pp. 27–55.

Strelcyn, Stefan *Catalogue of Ethiopic Manuscripts in the John Rylands University Library of Manchester*, (Manchester: Manchester University Press, 1974).

Taylor, F. 'The Oriental Manuscript Collections in the John Rylands Library', *Bulletin of the John Rylands Library*, Vol. 54 (1971–1972), pp. 449–478.

Trapp, J.B. 'Arabic Studies in the Warburg Institute', *British Society for Middle Eastern Studies Bulletin*, Vol. 8, No. 2 (1981), pp. 126–129.

Tritton, A.S. 'Catalogue of Oriental Manuscripts in the Library of the Royal College of Physicians', *JRAS* (1951), pp. 182–192.

Tuson, P. *A Brief Guide to Sources for Middle East Studies in the India Office Records*, (London: India Office Library and Records, 1982).

University College *The Gaster Papers*, (London: University College Library, 1977).

Vassie, Roderic (ed.), *Handlist of Arabic Manuscripts Acquired Since 1912*, 2 Vols., (London: British Library, 1994):
 Vol. 1: Islamic Law.
 Vol. 2: Qur'anic Sciences and Hadith.

Waley, M.I. (ed.), *Periodicals in Turkish and Turkic Languages: A Union List of Holdings in UK Libraries*, (Oxford: MELCOM (UK), 1993).

Wallenstein, Meir 'Genizah Fragments in the Chetham's Library, Manche-ster', *Bulletin of the John Rylands Library* Vol. 50 (1967), pp. 159–177.

Warburg Institute *The Warburg Institute*, (London: The Warburg Institute, 1995).

Wellcome Institute *Wellcome Institute for the History of Medicine: A Brief Guide*, 5th edn., (London: Wellcome Institute, 1993).

Young, J. & Aitken, P. Henderson *A Catalogue of the Manuscripts in the Library of the Hunterian Museum in the University of Glasgow*, (Glasgow: J. Maclehose & Sons, 1908).

Zedner, J. *Catalogue of the Hebrew Books in the Library of the British Museum,* (London: British Museum, 1867, repr. 1963).

Interested scholars and students may also find it useful to consult the pamphlet entitled *Middle East Libraries Committee (UK) Handbook,* issued by MELCOM (UK) in 1995.

Index

Page for Notes

For Product Safety Concerns and Information please contact our EU
representative GPSR@taylorandfrancis.com
Taylor & Francis Verlag GmbH, Kaufingerstraße 24, 80331 München, Germany

www.ingramcontent.com/pod-product-compliance
Lightning Source LLC
Chambersburg PA
CBHW050432280326
41932CB00013BA/2083

9 781138 981041